Songs From Life

A DEVOTIONAL INTRODUCTION TO THE PSALMS

*Volume 1: The Laboratory of Life
Psalms 1 Through 8*

ALSO BY RICK C. HOWARD

The Lost Formula of the Early Church
Strategy for Triumph
The Judgment Seat of Christ

WHAT OTHERS HAVE SAID ABOUT RICK HOWARD'S PREVIOUS BOOKS

"It may strike some as a super ficial generalization to say, EVERY CHRISTIAN SHOULD READ THIS BOOK, but that is exactly what I intend to say to my own congregation. They know I am neither reckless with words nor casual in my commendations. This book is a sobering summons to our souls — a sensitively discussed but starkly honest presentation which will **enrich** the reader."

Pastor Jack Hayford

"This message jolted me with a traumatic glimpse of eternity. It has shaped my life and rescued me from misspent years."

Author John Dawson

"It was a timely treat for me to be able to read Rick Howard's most recent book, *Strategy For Triumph: A Christian Perspective on Problems.* Rick has avoided theological "buzz words", and religious generalities. Someone once stated, "Pat answers are an enemy of progress." Rick has certainly stayed away from "pat answers…""

"I was impressed with his advice for troubled people to recognize that God has a practical discipline for everyone. If you have a pressure point and want to work through it, I suggest you read Rick's book and catch his progressive messages."

Evangelist Dick Mills

"I believe it is…the message on the heart of God for the Body of Christ at this point in history."

Loren Cunningham

"I read it with great interest. It is very moving."

David Wilkerson

Songs From Life

A DEVOTIONAL INTRODUCTION TO THE PSALMS

Volume 1: The Laboratory of Life
Psalms 1 Through 8

Rick C. Howard

Naioth Sound and Publishing
Woodside, California

Unless otherwise indicated, all scriptural quotations are from the
New King James Version of the Bible.

Songs From Life
Published by:
Naioth Sound and Publishing
2995 Woodside Road, Suite 400
Woodside, California 94062
ISBN 0-9628091-4-4

Cover design and book production by:
DB & Associates Design Group, Inc.
P.O. Box 52756, Tulsa, OK 74152

Editorial Consultant: Phyllis Mackall
                    Broken Arrow, OK 74012

"Where Am I Going"
(Cy Coleman, Dorothy Fields)

Printed in the United States of America.

Dedication

To the leadership and congregation of Peninsula Christian Center, Redwood City, California, who have been the loving anvil and arena of my ministry for 25 years and still counting!

Most Scripture speaks to us, while the Psalms speak for us.[1]

—Athanasius

Contents

The Laboratory of Life

SECTION 1

Reading and Relating to the Psalms

The Psalms model praise and devotion as they flow from the hearts of people who know the living God. They meditate upon God's majesty and respond to His intervention by giving Him glory. They ring with shouts and singing. They summon every living being and every human instrument into a choir of praise to the merciful and mighty God (Psalm 150). The renewal of the church begins in a renewal of worship. The Psalms will lead us into a deeper intimacy with our Creator and Redeemer and show us how to praise Him properly.[2]

—Donald N. Williams

The Psalms open up to us familiar access to God.[3]
—John Calvin

Preface

(Avoid This Preface at Your Own Risk)

*O*f all the books in the Bible, the Psalms provide us with the longest, steadiest, and deepest look into life. The Psalter stands unchallenged as the supreme expression of the human spirit in search of understanding and obeying the will of God; the human spirit struggling to relate God to every arena of life.

The Psalter is also the most democratic of all books. All men are at home in its pages, because it speaks a universal language ministering to universal needs. It is not a book of doctrine that divides and subdivides Christians; rather, it unites people of all backgrounds.

Chrysostom, an influential leader in the Early Christian church, once wrote:

> If we keep vigil in the church, David comes first, last, and middle. If early in the morning we seek for a melody of hymns, first, last, and middle is David. If we're occupied with funeral solemnities of the departed; if virgins sit at home and spin, David is first, last, and midst. In monasteries, among the holy choirs of angelic armies, David is first, middle, and last. In the convents of virgins, where are bands of them who imitate Mary; in the deserts where men are crucified to the world, and having their conversation with God, first, middle, and last is David.[4]

The Psalms provide a universal understanding and involvement with life. They form a stage where all men feel comfortable; a play with characters who are real and with whom we can identify. It is a book of the laboratory of universal human experience.

Perhaps that word "laboratory" provides a reason to discuss this book. There are already multitudes of volumes written on the Psalms. They include the critical, the scholarly, the devotional, and the explanatory. I have listed in the end of this book some of those volumes I have found most helpful. Why, then, this book? Why another effort to decipher the Psalms?

I have always felt a great urgency in my spirit that faith *in* God must become faith *with* God. Bruce Larson, the relational theologian, recognized this when he wrote, "I see a distinction between living a Christian life and living life as a Christian."[5]

So many of us carry our religion in a neat, tightly packed briefcase which we pick up on Sunday morning and bring to church. When we go home, we sit it in the corner and pick up our secular briefcase to carry throughout the rest of the week. We are easily caught up in "living a Christian life," but not in experientially "living *life* as a Christian."

The Psalms, however, contribute a different perspective on a believing FAITH-life. They express struggle and integrity as the experience of people who openly and honestly allow their experiences to be recorded without pretense. There is an experimental attitude in their honesty.

The most difficult and potentially embarrassing attitudes are vulnerably exposed, and even private, personal revelations are given if they shed light on the life-experience in general. Are the psalmists sadists — reverse voyeurs who take pleasure in saucy revelations? Do they stand by and wait a few centuries for the shock value of their recorded indiscretions or questionable attitudes to shock or disappoint?

The great value of the Psalms is that each writer wrote from his own experience. Here we see godly men transferring in a vulnerable way exactly how they are feeling, and it is done so that we might profit. It is right for us to regard their experiences as parallel to our own. In fact, if we don't read the Psalms in that way, one could question if we have read the book at all.

These writers are experiencing the experiences we do, and that's why there is a great spiritual bonding and identity for the person who understands this book. The Psalms teach by the process experience, not by doctrine or rote. They are not, in most instances, didactic or doctrinal in their presentation. The Psalms teach us simply and in reality.

Each psalmist says, "I went through this. This happened in the firestorm of my life. Let me share it with you." The Holy Spirit often turns the spotlight on our own lives from the vulnerable spirits of these people, and from their experiences comes forth a fresh vitality in our own faith.

Although I am not a physical scientist, I recognize a characteristic of science that unites the Psalms. Each writer has a hypothesis — a basic philosophy concerning life and a theology concerning God. Their experiences, then, become experiments.

The conclusion is less important than the exercise. What matters most is what was learned or felt. An experience with God is seen as a process. Therefore, everything is sacred, and nothing is secular — at least *simply* secular. The important element is the truth concerning each detail.

Like many scientists, the psalmist seems willing for posterity to work out the connection or figure out the results. He seems to be saying, "Here's my laboratory experiment with God. I want you to profit from this; to be encouraged by it. I want you to be strengthened by my experiences." Even more vulnerably, each psalmist seems to add, "I'm not really sure of the actual outcome."

This style, or approach, if you will, is most unusual compared with the almost trite, compartmentalized religious experiences of today. When is the last time you heard of a spiritual leader writing a song about his sin and having the choir sing it for the Sunday anthem prior to his own vulnerable and realistic discussion of what he has learned from the process of his experience?

Men and women who really know God struggle with their faith. Christian life is not all mountaintops of spiritual ecstasy or self-sufficient ease. Neither is it a stage of arrival or perfection where the believer is always "together," polished, or spiritual. We are meant to have a living two-way communication with God. Faith is a struggle, a laboratory, where we learn to change and really live in practical and vital reality.

Most people at one time or another have wonderful religious experiences. Yet we ourselves remain unchanged. When we tear through the phoniness of our experience, we find ourselves isolated. When we pawn the Christian life off as perfectionalism, a mystic experience, or a briefcase to be carried only on religious occasions, we are playing a dangerous, phony game which robs us of true relationships with others.

That's really the purpose of this book. Something is wrong when faith becomes creedal and exclusive. A repetitive message of the Psalms is that sin is not only hostile or overt acts of crimes; sin is also being unable to hear the person God has put next to you in life.

The Christian life, I believe, is meant to be a laboratory of vulnerable, transparent experiences with God and with fellow Christians. I defraud others when I bottle up an understanding of truth which has emerged through the brokenness of my life.

This study is indeed devotion. It can be fairly called experiential and relational. But it is more. There is here an honest, straightforward opinion or theory that the Psalms unite with a premise and strongly belie a purpose: They call for a conclusion; they are evidence which demands a verdict. And, like all truth, the Psalms are meant to affect life, not simply clarify positions or provide ground for debate. Otherwise, the costly laboratory experiments, faithfully and painfully documented, are useless.

Here's to vital life in the laboratory!

The Psalms are like manna which tasted to every man like that he loved best.[6]

—John Donne

CHAPTER 1

Give Me a "P,"

Give Me an "S," Give Me an "A"...

One of the most successful and resilient Broadway plays of all time is "The Fiddler on the Roof." Its central character is a middle-aged Jewish man named Tevye, who lives in a small, out-of-the-way Russian village. The story takes place toward the end of the 19th century.

This simple peasant has discovered something of the grace of God; something of the marvelous plan which God has for every man. Consequently, Tevye's whole life is a prayer — a real, honest, two-way communication with God.

On any day he may turn to God with complaints about the Russians, his family, the crops, or his business. Once he caps off his grumbling by muttering, "God, You say money's a curse. So curse me, just once, just a little bit!"[7]

For this Jewish peasant, life was a struggle, and his relationship with God didn't shield him from trouble or tragedy. Tevye is a psalmist, and that's what the Psalms are all about — taking religion from the shelf and putting it in earth shoes.

Many of the Psalms use acrostics as frameworks for their construction. An acrostic is formed when a writer takes a word and starts a different sentence or verse from each letter in the original word or list. Psalms 9, 10, 25, 34, 37, 111, 112, 119, and 145 are *all* acrostics.

In Psalm 112, after the opening "hallelujah," each line begins with consecutive letters of the Hebrew alphabet.

1

Psalm 37 has the same construction, except the consecutive letters are in every second double line.

The longest chapter in the Bible, Psalm 119, has 22 stanzas of eight verses each. Each line of the first stanza begins with the Hebrew "A," each line of the second stanza begins with the Hebrew "B," and so forth. There is some evidence that Samuel first developed this poetic method of instructing the young Hebrew yeomen both their language and their history in his early attempt at a national system of education.

I would like to borrow this simple, primitive method of learning — the acrostic — to provide some basic introductory material to the Psalms which I believe is both important and revealing. I will use the word "Psalms" itself to cover some issues that any student of the scriptures must learn. Like an earnest cheerleader, I want to encourage you with a fervent, "Give me a 'P,' give me an 'S,' give me an 'A'..."

The "P" in my acrostic stands for "Prayer and Praise." These words provide meaning from the Hebrew title of this book of Scripture. The word "Psalms" is not the original title; it is a simple Greek word meaning "songs." The original Hebrew title was *tehillum* or *sepher tehillim,* which means "praises" or "book of praises." Another Hebrew title — *tephilloth* — or "prayers" is given at the close of the second section of the Psalms.

Therefore, one can be correct in saying that the Psalms are a book of prayer and praise. The Book of Psalms is, in fact, the prayer book of both the Hebrew and the Christian traditions.

You have probably already guessed the meaning of my "S." The Psalms are obviously a book of "Songs" — songs born from real experiences in the laboratory of life. They are not theological or deep. They come from someone skipping through life. The psalmist sees God in melody and harmony. Only a psalmist could see mountains leap for joy or trees clap their hands!

As we have already mentioned, the English word "psalm" comes from the Alexandrian Greek word *psalmos*, which means "a poem that is sung to a stringed instrument." So it is a book of songs, and they are meant to be sung. These songs belong not only in the litany of the church or synagogue, but in the worship of every believer.

There is no more poignant scene in all theater than the scene where Tevye turns to his wife, his companion in the struggles of life, and asks, "Do you love me?"

She replies, "Do I love you? What a question! Who prepares your food and washes your clothes and scrubs your floors and shares your bed and raises your children?"[8]

But the response doesn't satisfy Tevye, so he asks again, "But do you love me?"

Again his wife mentions all the things she has done for her husband. But Tevye still presses the question: "But do you love me?"

Can you see the tragedy of this scene? Tevye felt isolated and needed loving, transparent assurance from his wife. But he didn't receive it! His experience left him isolated.

Are you getting comfortable with the process by now? The next letter is "A," and that means "Authors." A significant revelation of the laboratory aspect of the Psalms can only come from willingness to sketch out the "who" and "when" of this book.

Many Christians say they love God's Word, but they are not concerned enough to ask basic questions: Who wrote it, and what were the circumstances surrounding the writing? Indeed, the realities, vulnerabilities, and openness of the people in the Book of Psalms demand that I care enough to know who they were and what was happening in their lives which produced this expression.

The "L" for me is "Life" or "Laboratory" — the key principle we are examining in this study. My perspective will be radically different when I accept my experiences as a part of the process. Each experience, including the negative or unhappy, becomes a document to learn from and through which to change.

The "M" word for me is "Mirror." The Psalms are a marvelous mirror in which we can find ourselves. Whatever our emotion or feeling, whatever our longing or disappointment, we can come to this book and see ourselves.

What is reflected may not always be good, but it is always accurate. Several early Christian writers as early as the third century saw the Psalms as a mirror. John Calvin wrote that the Psalms had been that for him.

Let me end with an "S" to represent "Satisfaction." Sorrowfully, there are few truly contented and satisfied people in our society, even among Christians. One preacher declared that most Christians wear their corsets too tight and somehow believe bulging eyes to be the proper Christian demeanor!

I believe God wants us to have a livable, satisfying, honest, and vulnerable kind of lifestyle which is neither self-deceptive nor lived out in pretense. God wants us to have the deep satisfaction of fulfilled lives.

Preaching and teaching through the Psalms is to rediscover the prayer book of our lord Jesus Christ. We sense His presence as we underline verses that are prophetic of His life and death and as we see the forthcoming drama of the Atonement.[9]

—Lloyd John Ogilvie

CHAPTER 2

The Big Three

*(The Three Experiential Gates of
Praise Experience)*

'm sure you have listened to a speech or sermon, read a book, or watched a movie, only to conclude with frustrated questions: "What's the purpose?" "What's he trying to say?" or, worse yet, "I don't get it!"

In one of the famous "Peanuts" cartoon strips, that type of question is very much on Lucy's mind when she says to Charlie Brown, "I have a lot of *questions* about life, and I'm not getting any answers. I want some real, honest-to-goodness answers. I don't want a lot of questions. I want answers!" Charlie Brown's best reply was, "Would true or false be all right?"

The truth is that we are all too familiar with times when our spirit is too weary to receive more direct instruction; our heart is too bruised; and our mind is so tired we cannot be objective or concentrate upon principle.

The Psalms are of inestimable value in this respect. They don't preach at us or demand from us; instead, they provide wonderful arenas for comparison and ultimate release.

I believe there are three objectives the Holy Spirit has shown me about the Psalms. When I understand them, I am able to apply the Psalms to my life more specifically and in an experiential manner.

The Laboratory of Life

First, as we have seen, *the Psalms are to be seen as a laboratory of life — a living, continuing expression of hope and futility, of faith and despair, of joy and immanent pain. It is a laboratory of life from the first look, because in it we find godly but human men who state their experiences and give an actual account of things which have happened to them in their spiritual lives and their warfare.*

These are people who open up their lives and say, "Come on in and look. This is how faith has worked out in my experience. These have been my troubles and experiences, and I want my life experiment with God to be profitable and helpful to you."

Second, it is important to examine the circumstances. Each specific background to the circumstances or experiences of the psalmist while writing a Psalm is important. The most ancient of the Psalms was written 3500 years ago and the most recent, 2500 years ago, according to several reliable scholars. Yet the Psalms are as contemporary and as meaningful as if they had been written last week. We feel as though each writer was peeking over our shoulder and experiencing our own personal lives, although each of these psalmists lived centuries ago!

Every Psalm represents a separate composition, although some interrelate closely. Like the Bible itself, the Psalms are a compilation of many authors' works which range over a long period of time. These Psalms reflect great moments of Hebrew history and probably did not reach their final compiled form until sometime between 400 B.C. and A.D. 100.

Just who were these authors who wrote the Psalms? You have probably heard some ministers and teachers naively credit David with the whole book. In fact, these ministers and teachers often refer to "the Psalms of David." However, even the most generous accounting indicates that David wrote only a little more than 70 of all the Psalms.

8

A second giant among the psalmists was Asaph. In a sense, he was David's choirmaster in Jerusalem. These two men enjoyed a beautiful relationship which you can read about in First Chronicles 6 or Second Chronicles 29. Doubtless, Asaph drank from the spirit of David and wrote another 12 or 13 Psalms himself. History suggests that some Psalms credited to Asaph were obviously written after his death, which suggests that his family wrote them in his name. They understood the spirit which motivated Asaph. Obviously, they were a close community and lived in an intimate manner.

Another group of Psalms was written by the Korahite Levites, David's Temple servants. These men worked closely with the things of God and wrote about them. Another five of the Psalms were penned by Haggai and Zechariah, at least two by Solomon, and one perhaps by Moses.

More than 40 Psalms are listed as "anonymous." Perhaps a godly man of the Old Testament, Hezekiah, wrote these. He was born to an immoral father and a godly mother, and he rose to become king. He cleansed and purified the Temple, restoring worship of the true God.

You will remember him as the king who begged God for more years, not simply to extend his life, but to complete the job God had given him to do. Hezekiah is almost universally credited with valuable work having to do with writing some of the Psalms and compiling others.

Think of the men involved in this "laboratory of life" — David, Hezekiah, Solomon, the Korahite Levites, Asaph, Moses, Haggai, Zechariah, and Ezra. The latter served as a compiler of the Psalms.

When we walk into this "laboratory," we walk into the lives of these incredible men who knew God. They wrote from bitter experiences that tried their souls as well as moments of festive praise or overwhelming victory. At least 30 Psalms came out of the exile period in Babylon, another 50 from the Persian period, when Israel was under the heel of that savage oppressor. A third group of 20 Psalms was written during the Maccabean period, which was a terrible time for the people of God.

We Live in Community

Our second basic focus of the Holy Spirit, in addition to seeing them as a laboratory of life, is that *we must see the Psalms as a manifestation of true believers' community — the kind of community in which God wants us to live as believers — transparent, vulnerable, non-deceptive, struggling, open, evolutionary, and inviting.*

We have viewed the honesty with which the psalmists did not hesitate to tell us much about themselves. But their honesty and realism is what makes us so comfortable ourselves in the Psalms. None of us have gone to the Psalms without being happy and delighted at the honesty of them, because we identify with them so obviously.

"The laboratory of life," which is the Psalms, also contains the elements necessary for a true believers' community. Few churches are true believers' communities. The Psalms speak of the marvel of a transparent, open, inviting faith which is non-deceptive, even to oneself. The phrase "non-deceptive to self" should be emphasized, because many Christians live in this kind of deception.

Someone needs to raise the flag for a new kind of fellowship — a New Testament believers' communion which gives more than lip service to caring for others. The Bible says we are to receive one another as Christ has received us, for the glory of God the Father (Romans 15:7). No one can carry us personally to that place, but with God's help, perhaps this book can create a hunger in you for fellowship according to such biblical principles.

Dr. James R. Dolby, who taught psychology at Baylor University and has often written about struggling as a new creation in Christ Jesus, wrote a book some years ago called *I, Too, Am Man.* It is a psychologist's reflection on Christian experiences. Dr. Dolby wrote, "What this world is looking for is men and women who are honest with themselves and with life and with God; men who are not afraid to be themselves."[10]

The only hope for the Church in this society is in that kind of personhood.

A book which has greatly shaped contemporary American life is J. D. Salinger's *Catcher in the Rye.* Salinger, in the person of a young man named Holden Caulfield, places an epitaph across 20th century America. It reads simply, "Man is a phony!"

An entire generation has acted on this simple truth. But the Church cannot afford to believe such an epitaph. Consequently, the Church cannot turn her back on the world! How tragic it would be to wake up one morning and find church doors closed and a sign on them that read, "You don't understand yourselves or us; therefore, we have no need of you. Signed, The World." The Psalms suggest a truly alternative approach to believers' community.

Dr. Paul Tournier, another Christian psychologist who wrestled with meeting the world head on and still retaining a vital experience with Christ, wrote in one of his wonderful books, "What isolates the patient most of his life, whether it's a school boy or a housewife or a worker, is the very thing that isolates us the most — our secrets."[11]

Here is where the psalmists are so victorious. They write with such remarkable honesty and are not afraid to tell us the truth about themselves. The 73rd Psalm is a classic example where the writer, a man of God, confesses that his steps are slipping, and he is like an ignorant beast before God. What honesty!

I know nothing in a spiritual light more *discouraging* than to meet a person who gives the impression that he or she walks constantly on a mountaintop. There isn't one Bible character who lived that way. There is no "church face" in the Bible. Some of us even describe our best clothes as "Sunday suits" or "Sunday dresses."

We get up on Sunday morning, kick the dog, scream at the kids, fight with our spouse, and drive 20 minutes to church in total silence. Then, when we set foot on the church parking lot, we are suddenly smiling and saying, "Good morning, brother! What a lovely Lord's day. Isn't it good to be in God's house?" It's a wonder God doesn't strike us dead!

Bible characters never acted this way. They knew what it meant to be cast down and suffer grievous trouble. Many a contemporary saint in the middle of his pilgrimage has thanked God for the honesty of the writers of the Psalms.

All of us in our pilgrimage can find a place in the laboratory of these men's lives to identify with. The psalmists were fallible people like us, but they pulled the cloak from their lives and said, "As God did, come in and live with me. Come to my house."

God called David, the most prolific psalmist, "a man after my own heart." This is a unique and wonderful phrase: "a man after God's own heart"! However, David wasn't always a *good* man. I doubt if he would get the endorsement of any pulpit nominating committee if he were alive today. He might even be rejected as a student at a theological seminary.

He was, among other things, a thief, an adulterer, and a murderer — but David was a man after God's own heart! If we can't understand that, perhaps we will never reach the depths of God's love for humanity.

When David saw his sins, he admitted them before God. He made no defense of himself to God or man. But he not only confessed; he also believed. He believed he was forgiven, even though he was a sinner. The Psalms take us into that experience and open it up to us.

Bruce Larson, a wonderful 20th century clergyman and author, tells about a friend he used to check in with every morning. Bruce would call and say, "How are things going?" The two men would then have a friendly chat and go about their day's business.

One morning the man answered Bruce's question with the statement, "Terrible. I had a fight with my wife last night, and we went to bed not speaking to each other, sleeping back-to-back. This morning, though, she kissed me and said, 'Honey, I love you.' But I said, 'Well, I *don't* love you. I don't love myself, I don't love God, and I can't think of anybody I do love. But I'm going to pray this morning, and I believe somehow God is going to straighten me out, because He loves me, and He will make me able to love again. And when He does, I promise to put you first on my list.'"[12]

Bruce's friend might have been a writer of the Psalms. He wasn't trying to live a superimposed, overspiritualized life. He was being real. A psalmist says, "I'm angry with God. I wonder why He's so slow, and why He doesn't compensate the good. I wonder why the evil prosper. I'm frustrated!" Would to God that all of us could live with that kind of honesty!

Perhaps some of us will never experience the *real* Christian joy meant for us until we can say, "I don't love you, I don't love anybody, but I'm believing God to do a work in my life, and when He does, you will be first on my list." We need to blast ourselves out of the muck of phoniness in religious pretension and profession.

Let it be equally noted that until we as a Church are made up of these kinds of people, we won't satisfy the desire of a God who relates to men and women in their experiences. May we be known as a people who have something real to offer for a world without that reality.

A man named David Ignatow wrote in his poem, "Two Friends":

I have something to tell you.
    I am listening.
I am dying.
I am sorry to hear.
I am growing old.
    Terrible.
It is. I thought you should know.
    Of course. I'm sorry. Keep in touch.
You too.
    And let me know what's new.
Certainly. Though it can't be much.
    And stay well.

And you too.
And go slow.
And you too.[13]

The tragedy of this poem is that I hear this sort of conversation all the time. It's where most of us live, passing one another like ships in the night. That's why Jesus said, "By this shall all men know that ye are my disciples, if ye have love one to another" (John 13:35). Not by being doctrinally straight or theologically orthodox, but in that we have love. Church buildings throughout the world fill each Sunday with bleeding, dying, frightened people whom many believers never bother to hear. We pass them and say, "Keep well. Go slow. See you next Sunday."

In this book we are focusing on three foundational or experiential gates to the Psalms experience. We have already examined the honest, vulnerable expression of the psalmist himself in the honesty of his declaration, and, second, the manifestation in the Psalms of a true believers' community — transparent, open, and inviting.

Indicative of True Access to God

As our third gate of examination, I want to point to the Psalms as indicative of *a true approach and access to God — one which is freeing, non-hypocritical, and non-defensive — yet an approach which is repentant, non-orthodox, and always subject to change.* The Psalms are a textbook on the worship of God as a lifestyle, not a ritual.

I believe the Holy Spirit is asking us to move out of our seclusion, come down from our man-made mountaintop, and become a people whose lives can be laboratories for the world — a people who love and care. I'm not referring to loving souls. I think many evangelicals love souls and hate people! I've never seen a soul, but I'm surrounded by people. Bruce Larson quotes Ernest L. Stech in his poem, "That's My Soul":

That's my soul lying there.

You don't know what a soul is?
You think it's some kind of ghostly sheet-like thing you can
   see through and it floats in the air?

14

That's my soul lying there.
Remember when my hand shook because I was nervous in the group?
Remember the night I goofed and argued too much and got mad,
    and couldn't get out of the whole mess?
I was putting my soul on the line.

Another time I said that someone once told me something
about herself that she didn't have to.
I said that she told me something that could have hurt her.
And I guess I was asking you to do the same.
I was asking you to let me know you.
That's a part of my soul, too.

When I told you that my mother didn't love my dad and I knew
    it as a kid,
When I said that my eyes water when I get hurt even though
I'm thirty-four and too much a man to cry,
I was putting my soul out there in space between you and
    me.
Yeah, that's my soul lying there.

I've never met God.
I mean I've never met that old man who sits on a cloud with
    a crown and a staff and knows everything and is everything
    and controls everything.
But I've met you.

Is that God in your face?
Is that God in your soul lying there?

Well, that's my soul lying there.
I'll let you pick it up.
That's why I put it there.
It'll bruise and turn rancid like an old banana if you want
    to manhandle it.
It'll go away if you want to ignore it.

But if you want to put your soul there beside it, there may
    be love.
There may even be God.[14]

I really believe that's what it's all about!

Devotion, *in a word, is the conscious, habitual effort to look toward God.*[15]

—Harold A. Bosley

CHAPTER 3

How To Use a Mirror

*T*here is an imperative integrity in the Psalms. Believing life, faith in God, permeates every dimension, colors every experience, and explains every circumstance. There is no division between the sacred and the secular. The Psalms do reflect a wonderful, honest, and restorative fellowship, a community of openness and vulnerability. But they reflect something else as well.

The Psalms stand foundationally on a winsome, attractive, and freeing knowledge of God and His desired relationship with man. Until we as individuals are free to celebrate the grace of God in this manner, we must exist essentially alone. There cannot be a community of transparent, open, accepting, and loving believers until there are first individuals who have expressed personally the love, grace, and acceptance of God.

Perhaps that is why Jesus said essentially that we were to love our neighbors as we love ourselves, and why Paul wrote concerning church division and legalistic judgment:

Therefore receive one another, just as Christ also received us, to the glory of God.

Romans 15:7 *New King James Version*

Perhaps that quote is more "the rub," so to speak, than the answer. How did Christ receive you? How does He receive you? Perhaps theology is in a large measure the *precedent* to relationship. Does God love us only when we do well and receive us only when we're good? Then, of course, our relationship with Him will reflect that tension.

I once took my family to a marvelously entertaining musical based on the "Peanuts" cartoon characters. The actors portrayed Lucy, Charlie Brown, Snoopy, Peppermint Patty, and Linus. Snoopy was played by a young man who wore a white turtleneck, white pants, and white sneakers. But he grinned in a certain way so that by the middle of the play there was no question that he *was* Snoopy. "Peanuts" cartoon figures are real to us because they often express the dilemmas of our contemporary society.

In one cartoon strip, Charlie Brown, infamous "Everyman" of the 20th century, turns to Linus and says, "We critical people are always being criticized." And we all recognize that there's a wealth of philosophy behind those words!

No one can be a loving, open, responsive, receiving human being toward others when he himself feels that God gets up every morning to see how many kids He can kick out of the family. If our whole attitude is that God is condemning and down on human beings — if we constantly live in a tension as to whether or not we're saved, depending on how well we've performed — if we receive the love of God only conditionally ("If I'm good He loves me, but when I'm bad He doesn't love me"), we can never respond to other people in an unconditional, nonjudgmental way. It is from God that we must learn that *acceptance* does not necessarily mean *approval*.

We discovered in the last chapter that there were many psalmists, and David cannot be credited with penning the entire collection. Perhaps we should look at this matter of authorship from another angle. The second most prolific author after David was Asaph, with at least 12 Psalms to his credit and that of his family. Asaph was David's choir director. The Korhite Levites, who wrote another 11 or 12, were David's elite tabernacle choir.

These two collections, along with a significant number of individual Psalms, came from those in the direct community of worship which surrounded David and his family. So, although it is naive to credit David with writing all the Psalms, his spirit casts its shadow over a predominant amount of them. Certainly, David personifies both the psalmist as an individual of vibrant faith and the psalmist as a part of intimate spiritual fellowship and true believers' community.

The significance must not elude us. David's own vulnerable, yet faith-filled personal experience with God enabled him to walk out a relationship with others that was winsome and dynamic. The Psalms as a collection not only demonstrate a man's great faith; they demonstrate a man's full life and freeing interpersonal relationship.

Another way to illustrate this truth is through the superscriptions — those words or phrases written over many Psalms. In most cases, they are not simply annotations added by compilers or anthologists of the Psalms. These words were probably scribbled over the Psalm by its author or someone closely attached to his purpose.

Many of David's Psalms, for example, are assigned or dedicated to certain men. You will see, "A psalm of David to the Chief Musician," or "A psalm of David for Jeduthun" (the founder of a musical group in David's tabernacle). Another Psalm is "To the sons of Korah," and another one, "A song sung for the dedication of the temple." Some were simply assigned "To the choir leader." (I'm sure he was encouraged to get a Psalm and not a nasty note!)

If you look into the Psalms even more closely, you'll see they often include a scribbled word of explanation about the circumstance under which they were written. For example, one reads, "A Psalm of David which he wrote when he fled from Absalom his son." How could anyone read that Psalm without entering into that circumstance, which must have been one of the most horrifying circumstances of anyone's life — a son rebelling and leading a bloody revolution to overthrow his father! David scribbles a Psalm as he flees from Jerusalem or shortly thereafter, "This is a Psalm I wrote while I was fleeing from my son, Absalom."

Examine these words carefully: "To be sung to the Lord concerning the words of Benjamin," or "A Psalm of David, the servant of the Lord, who spoke the words of this Psalm to the Lord on the very day the Lord delivered him out of the hands of Saul." Another says, "A Psalm of David when he pretended to be insane before Abimelech, who drove him out, and he went out."

These phrases all speak about that type of relationship. The Psalms continually point to community. David could write these words describing every emotion and circumstance, including his sin, and ascribe the words to those among whom he lived out a believer's life in open and attractive relationship.

The Psalms, then, are really a mirror that reflects our struggle, realistically portrays our weaknesses, and points us to the correction that would beautify and edify our being. John Calvin said:

> This book I am wont to style an anatomy of all the parts of the soul, for no one will discover in himself a single feeling whereof this image is not reflected in the mirror of the psalms.[16]

Isn't that true? Down, up, exhilarated, high, low, depressed, angry with God, wondering whether He has forgotten His purposes — all those emotions are mirrored in the Psalms. In a great sense, *we all become a part of the psalmist's koinonia or fellowship group.* His transparency with his experience, his reflection of growth in crises, of faith transcendent through doubt, encourages us.

I'm at home with this psalmist, comfortable with his vulnerability, encouraged to be honest with my own experiences. The fourth century scholar and theologian Athanasius wrote:

> To me it seems that the psalms are to him who sings them as a mirror, wherein he may see himself and the emotions of his soul, and with like feelings utter them.[17]

The psalmist experiences and celebrates forgiveness and grace, and then extends such forgiveness and grace to others. Such a community of transparent, non-deceptive people, such a fellowship of openness and healing, must certainly be the heart-cry of every true believer, and it is also the answer to Jesus' recorded prayer for the Church in John 17.

Again, let us realize that many Christians do not know that kind of God-life. They live performance-oriented lives, believing that God's acceptance is based on a daily track record. We stumble over ourselves in an effort to find body life. Know that you will never find accepting fellowship among Christians who take a legalistic definition for their faith.

When I as a professional clergyman attempt to show a congregation that there is no special virtue in a man or woman because a gift of God abides upon him or her, there will always be a predictable reaction from some people. They want the pastor to be on a special level, above ordinary problems. Some have even said to me, "I don't want to know your problems! I want to believe at least somebody's living right. Don't we pay you to live right? Isn't that why you're our pastor — so we can at least have the comfort of knowing that *somebody* has his act together?"

I once read a testimony from a Christian professor of psychology in a great church-related university. He spoke of the roles we are forced to play and our conformity out of fear of personal rejection or loss of love.

"I often find it hard to be myself. I find it difficult, I am pressed to play many roles," he wrote, "— professor, counselor, husband, a special kind of Christian professional psychologist. Each role carries with it different, though many times overlapping, behavior patterns. If I try to break through the superficial social expectations of each role, I will be met with opposition from without and within."[18]

Actually, that's not much different for any of us. When we try to break out and be a person, we hear things like, "You'd better be careful," or "How could you say that and be a true Christian?" Perhaps the most classic response (most often behind our backs, after we've tried to be honest) goes something like, "He must be having problems in his spiritual life."

You see, this is the tragic manner in which people insist that we play the game or the role. Even our Christian service and our very motives are affected. We are not free to examine why we do what we do — even religiously or spiritually. Sometimes the real person emerges, shyly, sometimes hostile, sensitive, lonely, sinful, or perhaps capable of great virtue.

But what happens when a person tries to express this and tries to break out of expectations to be a real person? You know what happens all too often: The person becomes an object of our prayers in a manner of judgment. We consider him or her backslidden or at least dangerously close to it. The tragedy is that we are then caught in a web of dishonesty ourselves.

Our whole church world becomes a play. We have a "victory in Jesus" smile which we only use once every seven days. It's a special smile that says, "My act's together, God's wonderful, and this is Sunday, when I wear special clothes and a special face." That, of course, is not godly! It is *not* spiritual or biblical. But it *is* all too often what we have done in the name of "Christian."

Dietrich Bonhoeffer, the German theologian who was martyred for his faith in Jesus Christ by the Nazis, once wrote:

Many Christians are unthinkably horrified when a real sinner is discovered among the righteous. So we remain alone in our sin, living in lies and hypocrisy.[19]

What a tragic but true statement. The Church was meant to be a place where honesty could exist, and honesty with a reason and a purpose: honesty not to condone sin, or to make sinners comfortable in their sins, but to show the way out that comes through the kind of integrity which the Word of God shows us.

I believe God wants us to celebrate this love and grace as well as our forgiveness and acceptance. The world needs people who want to be agents of healing. Thankfully, there are a flock of people who want to be God's people in this world — people who are struggling to know how. They are struggling to be in tune — on key — and to sing their Psalm for others.

A number of the Psalms were written around one experience of David's and the people of God. It was an experience all of us must stare into as vulnerably as we look into any mirror. It is an imperative reflection for those who would live the believing life as a laboratory, testifying to open fellowship with a God of grace and among a community of committed and transparent believers.

The story, which takes three chapters in First Chronicles to relate, concerns David's efforts to return the Ark of the Covenant to Israel. The ark symbolized the meeting place between God and man, and it represents the sacrifice of Christ which reconciles us to God in peace through grace.

Having been lost to the Philistines, the ark, though returned to Israel, had been kept in a barn at Kirjath-jearim through the years of Samuel's judgeship and Saul's reign and the first seven or nine years of David's kingship — perhaps 70 to 80 years in all.

David genuinely hungered for reality and the presence of God. He also sought confirmation of his rulership and confidence for his people. So he sought to bring the ark to his new capital of Jerusalem. But he did it the wrong way! He set out to do this spiritual task in the flesh with a man-made concept, using a new cart like the Philistines had used.

A judgment from God resulted immediately, and David ended up offended and pouting. Eventually, the scriptures were searched, and God's way was rediscovered. The presence of God was to come on the shoulders of the priests. In came the Ark of the Covenant of God and Israel with great jubilation!

Let's be frank: That story is a lot like us! We want to be that kind of Christian; the kind of community that God desires. God rewards our motive and our purpose, but we must act by the Word. The answer to our hunger is not to be found in limitless humanism or selfism but in a consistent dependence on Christ, recognizing our weakness and His provision. The Psalms are meant to save us from many things through the vicarious experiences in their vulnerable record. Why should we try our own carts when we have David's transparent experiment to help us learn?

Of course, you know David finally brought the ark in. When he did, he started rejoicing and dancing before the ark in the sight of his people. His wife, Michal, shouted at him, "Come inside. You're making a fool of yourself out there!" Evidently he was wearing some kind of skirt which left him improperly attired from Michal's viewpoint. She thought he wasn't behaving like a king should.

But David said, "I can't stop. This is a personal dance before God." And he was wildly excited. David was celebrating good news. He knew his life proved him to be a sinner — he was hardly a man who would ever be elected by a pulpit committee — yet David was a man striving to know God and make Him known.

See him now celebrating wildly — dancing before the ark — because he has personally experienced this joy! Record that picture for posterity. It is a laboratory experience that can be repeated.

Over the years I have received many cards, letters, and phone calls from people, many of which I would never repeat and would just as soon forget! However, one such letter which came during a message much like this chapter captivated my spirit.

The writer, then relatively unknown to me, has subsequently become a friend. As I have watched him struggle with the pain of his spiritual weakness and the drive he possesses for spiritual intimacy, I have been reminded a thousand times of his words. They are prophetic and convincing. They are personal, yet strangely universal. They are the words of a psalmist:

> Your words last Sunday became music to my ears, and my spirit was dancing in the aisle. I was becoming intoxicated on

the fruit of life, and at once I wanted to dance in the aisle of forgiveness, allowing the congregation to see who I am.

But the dance seemed awkward, I felt like a ball in a pinball machine, continuously bouncing off the side. After giving thought to this, I could see that awkwardness in the transparent community you were speaking about. It is a vulnerable dance among believers sanctifying ourselves together as we prepare for the final joyful procession into the eternal city of God.

God is continually using you to put form to the promises He has given me. For the past many months, God has been promising me a life that I would delight in. The intensity of this truth has drained me as I have tried the impossible task of making sin, sin, and righteousness, righteousness.

My secrets have isolated me from others, but soon I will be able to dance honestly before others. This will be healing...but without Christ, no one can have the kind of life God has.

This world is a great sculpture shop. We are the statues, and there is a rumor going around the shop that some of us are going to come to life. I'm glad God is preparing me for the miracle of change. Not a change whereby I lose my identity, but one where I find it and become the original authentic self I was meant to be. This is the call of God upon me that I give witness to the world that God is life.

So, Rick, I'm dancing because He has provided the music, and I close with a great feeling of love for you and praise to the One who has brought us together.

David might have written that! A David did.

[1]Athanasius, as quoted by Lloyd John Ogilvie in *The Communicator's Commentary*, Psalms 1-72, editor's preface. Word, 1986, p. 12.

[2]Donald M. Williams, op. cit., p. 17.

[3]John Calvin, as quoted by Lloyd John Ogilvie, op. cit., p. 12.

[4]Chrysostom, as quoted in *The International Critical Commentary, Vol. 1, The Psalms*, by Charles A. Briggs. Scribner's, 1906, p. xciv.

[5]Bruce Larson in *No Longer Strangers*. Word, Incorporated, Waco, Texas. Second Key-Word Edition, May 1979, p. 14.

[6]John Donne, as quoted by Lloyd John Ogilvie, op. cit., p. 12.

[7]Joseph Stein et al., "Fiddler on the Roof." New York: Crown Publishers, Inc.

[8]Ibid.

[9]Lloyd John Ogilvie, op. cit., p. 12.

[10]*I, Too, Am Man*, James R. Dolby. Word Books, Waco, Texas, p. 8.

[11]*Escape From Loneliness*, Paul Tournier. Westminster Press, 1962, p. 44.

[12]Bruce Larson, op. cit., p. 74.

[13]Steven Dunning (et al., eds.), *Some Haystacks Don't Even Have Any Needles*. Poem quoted, "Two Friends," by David Ignatow. New York: Lothrop, Lee and Shepard Co., Inc.

[14]Ernest L. Stech, as quoted by Bruce Larson, op. cit., p. 38.

[15]Harold A. Bosley, *Sermons on the Psalms*, Harper and Brothers, 1956, p. 51.

[16]John Calvin, Preface to *Commentary on the Psalms*.

[17]Athanesius, *Epistle to Marcell*, pp. 10-12.

[18]James R. Dolby, op. cit., p. 5.

[19]Dietrich Bonhoeffer, *Life Together*. Harper & Row, New York.

The Laboratory of Life

SECTION 2

The Biblical Statement on Life's Potentials

The Psalms are like a skillful surgeon who, having gone through the skin, tissue, and bone of external events, finally lays bare the heart of religious experience itself.[1]

—Harold A. Bosley

Give me the making of the songs of a nation, and I care not who makes the laws.[2]

—Andrew Fletcher

SALM 1

Blessed is the man who walks not in the counsel of the ungodly, nor stands in the path of sinners, nor sits in the seat of the scornful;

But his delight is in the law of the Lord, and in His law he meditates day and night.

He shall be like a tree planted by the rivers of water, that brings forth its fruit in its season, whose leaf also shall not wither; and whatever he does shall prosper.

The ungodly are not so, but are like the chaff which the wind drives away.

Therefore the ungodly shall not stand in the judgment, nor sinners in the congregation of the righteous.

For the Lord knows the way of the righteous, but the way of the ungodly shall perish.

New King James Version

CHAPTER 4

A Strange Delight
(A Prelude to the Psalms)

_Y_ears ago, I was given a rare and valuable edition of the Psalms which was done by John Henry Nash, one of the best-known printers and artists in San Francisco. Mr. Nash printed this work as a tribute to the Jewish community of San Francisco. The work took him 10 years to complete, and it is done with lovely art work and set in Gothic (a specific typeface). But John Henry Nash's comments at the end of his monumental task are most interesting. He writes:

> And here ends the Psalms of the singer, David; a book done for the joy of the doing, by John Henry Nash, printer of San Francisco, who turned his hand to the work as occasion offered over a period of ten years...May you who have read herein be enriched from the wisdom of the royal code of Israel. May you share his abounding tenderness. May your heart take to itself the spiritual harmonies of this song. And if anguish come to your soul which, heaven forbid, may it be soothed to comfort by the recollection of these inspired words.[3]

Indeed, the Book of Psalms, more than any other book in all the Bible, is a book which unifies spiritual people of all religious traditions. Unity among believers is an exciting thing!

If the Psalms are, as we have suggested, a laboratory of life, then certain factors involved in a scientific method must hold true. _Of greatest importance to such a method is the organization of information and the proposal of a hypothesis._ Whether

33

you flunked physical courses in your life or not, you basically know what a hypothesis is. But just to be safe, let's consult a dictionary. A hypothesis is defined as "a set of assumptions provisionally accepted as the basis for reasoning and experiment and investigation."

According to one source, a hypothesis is "a comprehensive tentative explanation of phenomena which is meant to include all other facts of the same class, and which is assumed as true until there has been opportunity to bring all related facts into comparison." A hypothesis is a comprehensive tentative explanation of phenomena.

Life demands a hypothesis! No one can live life without an idea of what it is meant to be. Whether or not we passed freshman biology or high school physics, we are all, nonetheless, scientists — and we are scientists in this laboratory called life.

In a sense, we have been born into the experiment itself, and all of us at an early age began collecting data: electrical plugs shock us, dogs may bite us, mamas are soft, and some foods taste better than others. Eventually, that data leads us to make early and important life conclusions, such as, "I like ice cream better than spinach," "Daddies aren't very dependable," "I'm not very smart," or "I don't like dogs."

Eventually, those conclusions become even more critical and life-influencing. They become hypotheses which emerge and shape the very destiny of our lives. Some people live out their life believing that only the strong succeed; love is weakness; feeling is final; or life isn't all it's cracked up to be! We often spend the rest of our life attempting to prove the hypotheses that we arrived at early in life. Most of us labor daily to prove our hypotheses, such as, "Get all you can, and can all you get"; "Nobody's going to provide for you — you must do for yourself"; "Don't trust anybody"; and many more.

Every person, as a result of collecting this data, forms some hypotheses, and then they live them out. You, like all of us, have formed these hypotheses and lived them out: the fact that you are not too smart, or you are not too talented, or you are pretty, or you are handsome, or you are this or that; the fact that life is wonderful, or life is terrible; life cheated you, or life gave to you.

The first Psalm is really much like that. There is no title to this Psalm, though almost all of the remaining Psalms, certainly in the first section, have titles. Second, there is no assigned author. Thirty-eight of the 41 Psalms in what is called the first book of Psalms, are definitely ascribed to David. However, the compiler of the Psalms did not give David credit for the first one. Perhaps he didn't know who the author of this Psalm was. Perhaps the compiler himself was the author, and he was too timid or shrank from giving himself the prominence.

One writer suggests these Psalms were compiled late in Hebrew history, and the man who was compiling them, or the Temple scribes who were compiling this hymnbook, thought it natural that this new edition needed a preface, so they wrote this first Psalm as a kind of introduction to the book; and it singled out the one motif that runs through the Psalms from beginning to end.

Many of the Church fathers did not regard this as a Psalm at all. In fact, they believed the first Psalm was a short summary of all the Psalms; namely, that God has appointed salvation to the righteous and perdition to the wicked. You will discover that the first Psalm in the old manuscript was actually the second Psalm, because they really didn't believe that our Psalm 1 was a Psalm, but, rather, an introduction — a kind of compendium.

Jerome, writing in the third century, said that the Church fathers at that time believed Psalm 1 was "The preface of the Holy Ghost." What a dynamic expression! In this book, I want you to view Psalm 1 as a grand hypothesis of the Holy Spirit — supernaturally given revelation which you are being asked to prove in the laboratory of life.

That laboratory of life takes two forms. In a sense, there are two laboratories in which this grand hypothesis is to be proven: First, in the lives of these struggling, devoted, yet human and sinning men who transparently offered us these songs in the book of prayer and praise we call the Psalms; and, second, in the laboratory of your own life.

Here we have a practical, yet supernatural formula to test and to prove in the varied experiences of your own three-score and ten years. Psalm 1 is a hypothesis, a comprehensive, tentative explanation of the phenomena of life which is subject to your own personal observation. That is what I believe the Holy Spirit is saying to us now.

There must be a myriad of reasons why people go to church. Psalm 1 is like an invitation of God's Spirit to yours. It is a dare, a trial, or even a summons. "To what?" you may ask. Psalm 1 is offered as nothing less than an explanation of life itself; nothing less than a statement of the grand alternatives to life. Perhaps our familiarity with this Psalm makes it difficult to appreciate the full abruptness of the challenge in its words.

These are the words which I spake unto you, while I was yet with you, that all things must be fulfilled, which were written in the law of Moses, and in the prophets, and in the psalms *concerning me.*
—Jesus (Luke 24:44)

CHAPTER 5

Life and Experiments With Limits

Psalm 1

*T*here is a bit of humor in the academic community which suggests that in order to have a Ph.D. (a Doctorate of Philosophy), you must learn more and more about less and less until you know absolutely everything about nothing. (I don't suggest you say that too loudly to your more learned friends!)

It is true, however, as a principle of all scientific research, that we must limit the area or subject of our coverage. Psalm 1 begins by describing such a limitation. "The blessed man" is not just *any* man. The original language suggests a man among a thousand who lives for the accomplishment of the purpose for which God created him. *That* man among men is the subject of a specific limited focus: "Blessed is *that* man" rather than simply, "Blessed is *the* man." He is a man who lives with a theme song:

You are worthy, O Lord,
To receive glory and honor and power;
For You created all things,
And by Your will they exist and were created.

Revelation 4:11 *NKJV*

You will quickly see that a sharp line is drawn across Psalm 1. It is as though the Holy Spirit writes at the bottom of this Psalm the words, *"Choose you this day."* It is God's statement of what life is meant to be, what it can be, and what He desires it to be for His children.

With this formula or hypothesis in mind, read this preface of the Holy Spirit, remembering that it is both a preface to the Book of Psalms and a preface to life itself:

Blessed is the man who walks not in the counsel of the ungodly, nor stands in the path of sinners, nor sits in the seat of the scornful;

But his delight is in the law of the Lord, and in His law he meditates day and night.

He shall be like a tree planted by the rivers of water, that brings forth its fruit in its season, whose leaf also shall not wither; and whatever he does shall prosper.

The ungodly are not so, but are like the chaff which the wind drives away.

Therefore the ungodly shall not stand in the judgment, nor sinners in the congregation of the righteous.

For the Lord knows the way of the righteous, but the way of the ungodly shall perish.

Psalm 1 *New King James Version*

Now *there* is a hypothesis to live out and observe all the days of your life!

These people in the Psalms whose lives are to be placed under the microscope are from a specific breed of people who, although fallible creatures like the rest of us, are remarkably honest and above all desire to glorify God. Their honesty is dictated by a desire to show the contrast between themselves and God and thereby to glorify Him. For example, the psalmist in the 73rd Psalm quite honestly says, "My feet had almost slipped...when I considered the way of the unrighteous...." He begins that Psalm by saying, "God is always good to Israel."

Whether it is David, Moses, Solomon, Haggai, Zechariah, Jeremiah, Asaph, the Korhite Levites, or Hezekiah — these writers are all *that* kind of man; that special breed of person who, although writing in the ink of personal experience, consciously brings God into their experiences. In so doing, each psalmist finds that God will do for him what no one else can do.

God heartened them in their days of fear. God supported them under their awesome burdens. God guarded them against danger. God calmed them in their crises. But, above all and most important, is the fact that this true understanding of God unified these men as they came to understand the controlling purpose of life.

Some people think that talking about unconditional love and transparency will lead to approving undisciplined, lazy Christian lifestyles. But there is a great difference! The Psalms place a limitation on the subject. There is a presumed bit of knowledge. We are speaking only about a man who has already focused himself on the ultimate purposes of God.

The Observance

The second rule of the laboratory experiment which develops from this hypothesis or preface of the Holy Spirit is that a man who seeks God's glory — who understands and surrenders to God's purpose — *that man will have a marked and observable difference in his life.* Nothing is clearer in the Word of God.

Believers will not always think the same about cultural issues of dress or so-called worldly amusements. They will never all look alike, act alike, talk alike, or even be found in identical circumstances. But one thing will always be true: *That* man will be blessed, happy, fortunate, and prosperous — not perhaps in the world's idea of prosperity, but with an enviable peace and joy of spirit.

Interestingly, the word "blessed" is actually a plural Hebrew word which means "blessednesses." It implies all the multiplicity of blessing which rests upon the person whom God has justified. "Blessed" might as well be translated "happy." It is not coincidental that the preface of the Holy Spirit to the Psalms begins with the word "blessed," the same preface Jesus' teaching ministry took in the Sermon on the Mount — blessed, happy, together, and unified.

41

Someone has suggested that a good translation of this first verse might be, "Hail to the man" or "Congratulations to the man." This kind of man has great reason for gladness and may be fittingly congratulated. "Congratulations! You've grabbed the gold ring! You've won the jackpot! You've guessed the secret number!" Oh, the blessedness to such a man!

Clare Boothe Luce, a brilliant 20th century writer and politician, wrote a marvelous short article on the meaning of the Fourth of July. Mrs. Luce was then a U. S. Congresswoman from Connecticut. In this article is a phrase about "believing people" which needs to be remembered. She writes, "For a people, as for a person, believing is *all*. All history bears witness that it is *the believers* who win the revolutions; it is believers who found the nations, who conquer the oceans, who tame the wildernesses, who raise up the great cities and the great institutions." She concludes, "The doubters, the cynics, the unbelievers, they can scarcely shake the pebbles from their shoes, much less move mountains."[4]

What a picture! Oh, the blessedness of those who are plugged in to purpose. That's a hypothesis of life the Holy Spirit suggests for you!

Niels C. Nielsen Jr., who has carefully researched the writings of Aleksandr Solzhenitsyn, finds an evangelical commitment by the famous Russian writer. Here is one of Solzhenitsyn's prayers:

How easy it is for me to live with you, Lord. How easy for me to believe in you. When my spirit is lost, perplexed, and cast down, when the sharpest can see no further than the night, and know not on the morrow what they must do, you give me a sure certainty that you exist, that you are watching over me, and you will not permit the ways of righteousness to be closed to me. Here on the summit of earthly glory I look back astonished. On the road which through depths of despair has led me here to this point, from which I can also reflect to men your radiance, and all that I can still reflect you shall grant to me, and what I shall fail, you shall grant to others.[5]

That's Psalm 1. That's the issue we are talking about — that kind of man, comfortable with God, comfortable with God's purposes, and thus unusually blessed in his personhood.

The Incomparable

Another note of this Holy Spirit hypothesis is that you must know that, as in all experiments, *there must be comparisons*. Scientists call this part of the laboratory experiment variables and constants. Contrast is often necessary for us to really see truth. Psalm 1 is in itself the most simple, yet the sharpest, contrast between godly and ungodly men which exists in the world.

The Holy Spirit stands these types of persons up, testifying first to the protection, joy, and blessedness of the one who trusts and knows God and believes in God's purpose for his life. Then the Spirit contrasts the picture with the ungodly, who are blown away like chaff, unable to stand at the Judgment or to be a part of the congregation of the just. What a contrast!

Let's continue to examine this "special kind of man." We are going to see a lot of them in the Psalms, for the Psalms are full of them. You see, this preface of the Holy Spirit becomes an epitome of the whole book. This man isn't perfect, and doesn't have his whole act together, but he possesses the proper attitude toward God. He lines his life up with the purposes of God, although altogether human. Thus, he is happy and draws "Hail to the Chief" from the crowd who watches his life. See him first in this Psalm as to his choice, his character, and then his condition.

Most photographs have a positive and a negative. X rays, in fact, are negatives. The X ray reveals the inner structure; it is not the positive image we are used to looking at. Limiting ourselves to X rays would be like having a friend pull out a photo album only to discover it was filled with negatives. The friend might say, "Now, if you hold it up to the light just right, you'll see that's Aunt Susie." There is not a positive image in the whole book — they're all negatives!

Our whole emphasis cannot be structure without the positive image. Christians can't always go around saying, "See my bone structure? I'm solidly built inside." What a tragedy! It doesn't attract the world; it repels the world as much as a skeleton in the closet would repel a visitor. Structure is necessary, and the negative is a part of the picture, but that must be from God's sight, not ours.

The negative of Psalm 1 is interesting when it describes this man, because it says, "He walks not in the counsel of the ungodly, nor stands in the path of sinners, nor sits in the seat of the scornful." Notice the progression of the negative: *walk, stand, and sit.*

Many people think backsliding is easy. You are serving the Lord one day, you do something wrong, and suddenly you're backslidden! Their whole life consists of walking a tenuous, difficult line. They think if you step off, you're lost.

The truth is that backsliding is infinitely difficult if you are a believer. God the Holy Spirit will do everything in His power, and throw every obstacle possible in your way, to prevent you from backsliding because He loves you. You are His child, and He will do everything to make the "slide" a miserable trip! You see, it's progressive. It doesn't happen overnight.

This believer of Psalm 1 doesn't walk in the counsel of the ungodly. Being attracted to the ideas of the world is the first step downward. The use of walking shows a kind of casual stroll into the world to look once, and walk back *out* again. The world's ideas — its music, its materialism, for example — present a danger. A believer is destined for ultimate misery when he believes and listens to what the world sees as important! We cannot walk in the counsel of ungodly men and be happy.

As someone wisely said, when the Holy Spirit is within you, you are really in trouble if you try to be carnal, because you can't even sin and have fun anymore! That's why some Christians are so miserable. There's not *enough* God in them to fully go God's way, yet there's *too much* God in them to go the world's way. They are miserable either way. They don't like church or Bible study. Their eyes are on their watches every Sunday morning. Yet when they sin, they are also miserable. They are unhappy people! "Blessed is the man who doesn't walk in the counsel of ungodly men, *nor stand* in the way of sinners!"

There's an interesting word. The word "stand" is often used in the New Testament. For example, Paul says in Romans 14, "God is able to make him *stand.*" Paul also writes, "Having done all, *stand.*" It's a word which speaks about a contemplated definite decision to take your identity with a certain point of view or philosophy.

The psalmist says in Psalm 1 that after a man has *walked* too far in the counsel of the ungodly, he begins to stand in the way of the sinner. He takes his *stand* with them. He participates in their worldly society. Then, the Psalm continues, he eventually *sits* in the seat of the scornful. He takes his Ph.D. in worldliness and becomes a master of spiritual deception. Now *that's the negative* — the negative choice this man makes. The Spirit says, "Blessed is that man" — that specific man — who is in union with God, and who will *not* walk either in the counsel nor stand in the way of the sinner. Neither will he in any way sit with the cynic and the skeptic.

His Choice

The important part is the positive: "But his delight is in the law of the Lord, and in His law he meditates day and night." The law? What does that mean? The law to this man is a reflection — a portrait — of God's purpose for man. That law is not a burden. It is a delight!

The New Testament clearly teaches that no believer is *under the law,* but a believer has the privilege of being *in* the law of God. "Who delights..." without negative acquiescence or forced condescension. This person's joy is to know what God's joy is. This person delights to think God's thoughts after God and is excited to be a part of spiritual things. He not only delights in them, but he meditates on them both day and night.

Meditation is an interesting thing. It must not be confused with so-called Transcendental Meditation. In Transcendental Meditation you turn your mind off, and, by incantations, involve wrong supernatural activity! It's not Bible meditation. The Hebrew word for meditation means to cogitate, like a cow chews her cud. It means to take a verse of scripture and think about it, swallow it, and bring it up to chew again and again. Take one verse for the whole day and perhaps another for the night.

Another close definition would be "to chatter about it." It's a word that has the concept of talking, attention, and involvement. This psalmist is someone you will readily know, because he delights to talk about the things of God. We all enjoy chattering, but what we chatter about makes a lot of difference.

"That man" meditates. Perhaps "day and night" refers to two kinds of experiences, although nights can be very difficult for people who suffer from insomnia. The Word of God has a great effect on our lives if we meditate on it at night, taking a word from the Psalms or other scriptures, and as our last waking thought, placing our attention upon that thought from God's Word.

But couldn't "day and night" mean something else — *day* speaking of the brightness and joy of our experience and *night* of the sorrow and suffering of our experience? If so, this kind of man will not buy the counsel or companionship of the world. He positively enjoys and delights himself in God's way, and he constantly talks and thinks about both "in day" and "in night" experiences.

That positive note of discernment about this characteristic man must be a particular emphasis for us. This man who in a way personifies the Psalms is a struggler. He doesn't have his act together. He sins and knows it, confesses, and repents in honesty. He doesn't always understand, nor does he always agree with what God is doing; nonetheless, he is a

man with a strange delight. The delight described in this passage is to delight after the law of God. How strange that
sounds to our ears! To many, the law is a sorrow, hindrance,
and shackle. It restricts, denies, and inhibits us. Law either
compels us or disciplines us.

A. E. Housman, a great poet, expresses the attitude of
the majority of the world when he writes:

The laws of God, the laws of man,
He may keep that will and can,
Nor I; let God and man decree
Laws for themselves and not for me;
And if my ways are not as theirs
Let them mind their own affairs.[6]

That quote really represents the contrast. The psalmist
delights in the law of God.

And what is the law of God? There are perhaps three
areas of thinking here. First, the psalmist sees an orderliness
of everything God has made. It is all made with a magnificent
purpose. That's the first thing the psalmist obviously means
by "the law of God." What atheist, agnostic, or even cynic or
rebel would you hear saying:

**The heavens declare the glory of God; and the fir-
mament shows His handiwork.**

**Day unto day utters speech, and night unto night
revels knowledge.**

Psalm 19:1,2 *NKJV*

Or,

**What is man that You are mindful of him, and the
son of man that You visit him?**

**For You have made him a little lower than the
angels, and You have crowned him with glory and
honor.**

Psalm 8:4,5 *NKJV*

Or these marvelous words:

**When I consider Your heavens, the work of Your fin-
gers, the moon and the stars, which You have ordained.**

Psalm 8:3 *NKJV*

I'm sure you see the difference. The law of God to the psalmist is founded on creation. God has made all things, but not in some deistic creation where He later backed away and went to sleep, letting everything work its way out toward final destination. God made it all to have a purpose. It's all part of His plan, and that's the law of God in which the psalmist delights.

But the psalmist also delights in God's *involvement* in human history. He declares a divine providence. God is involved with His people. He is doing something. He is acting, fighting the enemy, building up and tearing down. God establishes. He is involved. The law of God is that He now has an interest.

Prayer has become rote, even to some Christians. They cannot accept a God who by prayer becomes intricately involved in the providence of history. What a tragic dichotomy — an *inactive* living God!

But the psalmist's delight also includes the revelation that God makes in His holy Word. God expresses Himself; He is not silent. The five books of the Law, the prophets, and the message of the wisdom literature, with the glorious New Testament, abound with truth. This man is a person who delights in the law which God has revealed. That is the choice of this kind of man. He chooses not to walk in the counsel of the ungodly, nor to stand in the way of sinners, nor to sit in the seat of the scornful. Instead, he *chooses* positively to delight in his inner man, after the presence and revelation of the law of God, and he meditates on it day and night.

His Character

It's an aphorism that we are what we think. We become what we dwell on. The description beginning in Psalm 1:3 seems simplistic but radiant:

He shall be like a tree planted by the rivers of water, that brings forth its fruit in its season [timely and accurate]**, whose leaf also shall not wither; and whatever he does shall prosper.**

Psalm 1:3 *NKJV*

What a fantastic description!

This tree has been *planted.* It is not wild growth or something which just happens to exist. It is not unplanned development. This man, like this tree, is domesticated, chosen, and elected. God planted him, and that's always an amazing truth: divine election! No one can ultimately believe that salvation is a result of man's decision. God has chosen. That choice of God is a scheme of faith-righteousness which certainly demands the cooperation of the human spirit. It demands both to make that election and calling sure. But the point is simple. God chose it.

You are something special — chosen and planted like this tree! A righteous man is like that. He isn't a fallen, wild sprout growing up and depending on the elements. He is cultivated, chosen, and planted by the Holy Spirit. If you are a believer, it's because of God's work. As the Bible says:

just as He chose us in Him before the foundation of the world, that we should be holy and without blame before Him in love.

Ephesians 1:4 *NKJV*

What does that say to you? To the psalmist, the fact that he's chosen and planted means that God is going to see to it that this life flourishes.

Years ago, we purchased an older house. All the yards had to be replaced, old plants ripped out, soil cultivated, and new plants chosen. I discovered something important: I am concerned about the plants I bought and planted myself. I chased away any dog in the neighborhood who threatened those plants. Why? I have a personal investment in the plants. Here the psalmist realized that God had planted that tree. And don't forget that God places His planting beside the rivers of water.

In the original language, this is not "river" as we might think of it. This is the word in the Hebrew for "those rivulets," or designed irrigation ditches, which the owner of a vineyard specifically cuts through the ground to enable water to flow freely to that vineyard, or, in this case, to that tree which he has planted. God has planted this tree in Psalm 1 by a multiplicity of these channels. If one fails, there's another! The truth must be applicable to us. God has provided diversities of supply in our life. Some will fail, and this is always difficult for us.

The Word of God is a wonderful channel, but there are times when it may seem to dry up. Sometimes when you read the Scripture, it is as dry as dust. There are times we come to it in an act of sheer discipline. Thankfully, most times it abounds. You open it, and it leaps at you full of life and promise. But when that river may not be quite as nourishing as you want, for whatever reason, there are other rivulets. There's the river of grace, when we've sinned and fallen short of God's purpose; the rivulets of forgiveness, mercy, confession, and prayer. Just imagine, all these divine rivulets are running right where God has planted this tree. He has provided everything needed for this tree to be fruitful.

In fact, this tree, planted by these rivulets of life, is known by two things: It bears fruit in its correct season, and its leaves do not wither. Now that's the best of two worlds! We have marvelous evergreens in the area where I have spent much of my life. However, they don't bear fruit. But here in Psalm 1 is an evergreen tree that is a fruit-bearer! This, by the way, is one of many descriptions of this very tree which we're going to see in the eternities of God, in the heaven of heavens, and in the New Jerusalem.

What does "fruit in its season" mean? Perhaps it's as simple as this: The fruit God expects in the particular life cycle or season of that tree. All of us can boast when things are going well, "I have great patience. I'm a patient Christian." But perhaps God says, "But that's not the fruit you need for now. When you're in *tribulation*, the fruit is patience."

Someone else might say, "I have great joy. I've never been happier in my life than I am now. Things are going great!" God says, "That's wonderful, but joy isn't the fruit for this season. Joy is the fruit at the time the grapes are being crushed — when things *aren't* going good." When things are going great, the fruit God is looking for is stewardship.

I wish I could tell you how many men have said to me, "If God would only prosper my business, if things would only go better. Pastor, I want you to agree with me that things will get better. When they do, I'm going to do thus and so for the Lord." God *does* prosper them. And what happens? Everyone seems willing to give the fruit of stewardship when we don't have anything. "Oh, I'd gladly give a tithe, pastor. I just don't have anything." Then God gives to us. That's when He expects the fruit of stewardship — fruit in its correct season.

Perhaps one of the hardest things to do is to *rejoice with those who rejoice* when you yourself are suffering. It's easier to suffer with the suffering in a kind of condescending manner, thinking, "Everything's going well with me, and he's suffering — poor thing."

When a believer comes to church saying, "Praise God, things are wonderful," and we're down in the dumps, we're tempted to say, "Brother, you wouldn't think things were wonderful if you'd gone through what I did this week," rather than saying, "Oh, yes, I'm so glad for you. Isn't it wonderful that these good things are happening to you!" Fruit in its season — and a leaf that doesn't wither — what a desirable state!

Have you heard the favorite American expression, "Hurry up and wait"? Most of us are rushing somewhere, and we don't enjoy getting there at all. Once we get there, we turn around and come back, and we don't enjoy *that* trip, either. What a tragedy!

This man who is at one with the purposes of God, although far from perfect, possesses a blessedness and a holy sense of togetherness. The blessedness God has dwells in a man who makes these kinds of choices both negatively and positively, a man who has this kind of character and foundation. God the Holy Spirit calls and purposes something in our laboratory of life experience that will confirm and establish a life-changing pattern.

A story is told about a group of Americans who were making their way through Africa. At a seaport, they employed a group of natives to lead them through that country. They told their guides that they were in a great hurry, which is not at all unusual for Westerners. The first day they went through the jungle at a rapid pace. They continued their relentless pace throughout the second day.

Finally, on the third morning, when the Americans were hurriedly preparing for another day of rapid travel, they found their native guides squatting under some trees, refusing to move. Bewildered, the Americans asked the natives why they were not ready to start. The spokesman said simply, "We shall rest today to let our souls catch up with our bodies."

Life does not end here. It's going somewhere. The God who gave it has a purpose for it. Without living by that purpose, a person will never know what life is about. There can be no blessedness to life lived outside God's eternal purpose. What's more, God loves us. More than anything in the world, God wants each of us to stand still until our soul catches up with our body. He wants us *together* and *fruitful*. Furthermore, God wants us to benefit from all the blessedness He has to give. However, God will not run fast enough to overtake us if we insist on going the wrong way!

Hearing the report, they lifted their voices in a wonderful harmony in prayer: "Strong God, you made heaven and earth and sea and everything in them. By the Holy Spirit you spoke through the mouth of your servant and our father, David:

> *Why the big noise, nations?*
> *Why the mean plots, peoples?*
> *Earth's leaders push for position,*
> *Potentates meet for summit talks,*
> *The God-deniers, the Messiah-defiers!*

Acts 4 *The Message*

 $\mathscr{P}$SALM 2

Why do the nations rage, and the people plot a vain thing?

The kings of the earth set themselves, and the rulers take counsel together, against the Lord and against His Anointed, saying,

"Let us break Their bonds in pieces and cast away Their cords from us."

He who sits in the heavens shall laugh; the Lord shall hold them in derision.

Then He shall speak to them in His wrath, and distress them in His deep displeasure:

"Yet I have set My King on My holy hill of Zion."

"I will declare the decree: the Lord has said to Me, 'You are My Son, today I have begotten You.

Ask of Me, and I will give You the nations for Your inheritance, and the ends of the earth for Your possession.

You shall break them with a rod of iron; You shall dash them in pieces like a potter's vessel.'"

Now therefore, be wise, O kings; be instructed, you judges of the earth.

Serve the Lord with fear, and rejoice with trembling.

Kiss the Son, lest He be angry, and you perish in the way, when His wrath is kindled but a little. Blessed are all those who put their trust in Him.

NKJV

CHAPTER 6

Rebellion Is in the Genes

(Learning To Avoid the Avalanche)
Psalm 2

*T*he task of bringing God's Word to the average Christian in our society is difficult. Perhaps that partially explains why the division between heavy, scholarly discussion of the scriptures versus extremely personal and experiential Christian literature is so marked. There seems to be little sound biblical study in between.

In this book, we have set out to be honest and consistent with the scriptures and scholarship but personal and experiential with the application. It is my conviction that to be accurate, personal application must flow out of a realistic understanding of the Scripture itself. Further, when one undertakes such an understanding, although it is time-consuming and sometimes difficult, the end result is rewarding beyond description.

We all come to the scriptures with our own "glasses" or "lenses," so to speak; therefore, we are all influenced in making our own conclusions.

A funny story comes to us from a Sunday School teacher's effort to relate the story of the miracle of Jesus' feeding thousands of people with a small supply of bread. To test her skills, she asked the children to draw a picture of the event she had explained.

One little girl drew 12 persons carrying baskets filled with bread and fish — but wearing hair ribbons. "After all," the little girl explained, "they're the waitresses." Another girl finally gave up on her picture, which showed Jesus with a bread knife cutting up the loaves. "I can't make the slices thin enough," she complained. But the classic was a drawing of a big box-like object with a door handle placed to the side of the crowd. When the teacher asked, "What is that?" the little boy replied simply, "It's the freezer for the leftovers."

However we cut up the pieces, we must attempt to understand the Scripture before it becomes a workable experiment in our personal laboratory of life. Allow me to set that kind of stage for you now for Psalm 2.

In many ancient manuscripts of the Bible, Psalms 1 and 2 are together. They are one section or one preface, as we have already noted in the chapter on Psalm 1. In other early manuscripts, however, Psalm 1 is a preface, and Psalm 2 becomes Psalm 1. Either way, there are some things about Psalms 1 and 2 that are obviously alike: Neither has an author named, and neither has a title.

There is, of course, a specific reason in the Holy Spirit's provision for that. Psalm 2, like the first Psalm, deals with the major subject of the entire Book of Psalms, so it is a preface or introduction. In Acts 4 we find a New Testament indication of the author of Psalm 2. Inspired by the Holy Spirit, New Testament believers named David as the author.

Our next question might concern the time this Psalm was written. Apparently it was written after David brought the Ark of the Covenant into Jerusalem, because the Psalm specifically mentions the holy hill, Zion. That reference had to do with David's reign, which would have been about 1040 years before Christ. This time is one of the most familiar in Old Testament studies.

Briefly comparing Psalms 1 and 2, we find both discuss the antagonism of righteousness and wickedness. Yet there is a distinct difference as well. In Psalm 1, righteousness and wickedness are personified in people, through individuals. Psalm 1 is about that righteous man who does not stand in the way of sinners, nor sit in the seat of the scornful. His delight is in the law of the Lord, and the rest follows. That Psalm, you will recall, ends by comparing the wicked who, like chaff, are blown away with the righteous. The ungodly do not receive the blessedness of the righteous.

I am told that the original Hebrew repeats itself in verse 4, saying, "The unrighteousness are not so, not so the unrighteous." That repetition seems to say that there is no way the unrighteous will have this kind of life described in Psalm 1.

In Psalm 1, we are dealing with *individuals*. In Psalm 2, we are dealing with *kingdoms*. The issue is light and darkness, or powers which are engaged in unyielding conflict. This Psalm is also compared with Psalm 1, because the man of Psalm 2 is specifically God's king, the glorious Messiah whom God will reveal. The man of Psalm 1 is like a preliminary description of the character of a man after God's heart: a perfect man. Again, the specific subject, like the conclusion, unites the Psalms.

But allow me to quickly trace a third comparison. Psalm 1 is a general discussion about our duty. It is about the moral implications of righteousness in a man's life. Psalm 2, however, is about the *Savior*. It is an almost evangelistic Psalm and, in fact, has an altar call at the end!

There is, of course, yet another specific comparison between these two. You will quickly see that Psalm 2 is exactly twice as long as Psalm 1. The first Psalm begins with blessedness and ends with the curse upon a man's choice of unrighteousness or ungodliness.

Psalm 2 begins with that spirit of rebellion to God much like the end of Psalm 1 and ends with the verse that says, "Blessed are all those who put their trust in Him." So there is, as it were, a beginning and an ending of blessedness and a continuation through the center of the discussion of rebellion against God. Again, there seems an inevitable unity between Psalms 1 and 2.

But let us not proceed further without specifically acknowledging that Psalm 2 is a Messianic Psalm. It is about the Messiah; there is no doubt about it. Even Jewish scholars who do not acknowledge the Messiah as Jesus Christ have had little doubt about the fact that Psalm 2 is Messianic. The early Hebrew writers and scholars all attributed it to the Messiah; some of them in very dramatic ways. One such early Jewish writer specifically wrote about this long before Christ came, saying:

> Like a robber who was standing and expressing his contempt behind the palace of the king, and saying, "If I find the King's Son, I will seize him, and kill him, and crucify him, and put him to a terrible death," but the Holy Spirit mocks at it, and saith, "He that dwells in the heavens shall laugh."[7]

How prophetic were the words of that ancient writer. But this Psalm is not Messianic simply because ancient scholars so describe it, but because in the middle of this Psalm are two expressions which could only be Messianic: "You are My Son, today I have begotten You." Never could that be ascribed to David or any other earthly king.

There is another phrase which could only apply to God's Messiah. Psalm 2 declares that all the nations and all the heathen will worship and ascribe honor to this king. That never happened to any earthly king. It will only be given to the Messiah.

You should also know that Psalm 2 is quoted *seven* times in the New Testament. Those quotations tell us in a specific way what the character of this Psalm is all about. There are four specific stanzas, each with three verses.

Interestingly, the stanzas are not only on different subjects, but they are different speakers in each case. The exception is that the first speaker is the psalmist himself, as is the last.

Certain critical words which you should be aware of also appear in this Psalm. The word "anointed," for example, in verse 2 is the same word as "Christ." The word *Christos* in Greek is a translation which means "the Anointed" or "the Messiah." Obviously, that's not just a name. When we say "Jesus Christ," we are in fact saying "the Messiah," or "Jesus is the Anointed One of God." This is a specific Messianic promise.

Without belaboring a point, you will notice in verse 3 that the rebellion among the rulers is stated: "Let us break *Their* bonds in pieces and cast away Their cords from us" *(NKJV)*. Some Jewish writers a thousand years before the time of Christ saw clearly the implications of these words.

Though fiercely monotheistic, these writers saw that the psalmist was describing the Lord and the Anointed or Son as one. Certainly it would be wrong to ascribe to these writers an understanding of the doctrine of the Trinity we use today, but clearly and with integrity they saw the prophetic implication of that union.

The first division of Psalm 2 concerns this confederacy or rebellion against Jehovah and His Christ. The issue of the rebellion begins with an eloquent "Why?" It is as a sense of unbelief for the writers.

The psalmist is saying, "For what purpose — what could be the reason why men would so blindly rage against the purposes of God? What is there that brings this self-will and rebellion to the place that the nations oppose God?"

The applications of this are obvious. From the moment God spoke man into existence and gave him an ability to choose, man has had a tendency to choose wrong! Lucifer was the anointed cherub that covered or stood in the presence of God as an angel of authority. Yet he desired to be *as* God, and he was flung under the Earth for his rebellion. When man was created, God gave him every blessing possible and only closed off or limited one area, saying,

> **but of the tree of the knowledge of good and evil you shall not eat, for in the day that you eat of it you shall surely die.**
>
> **Genesis 2:17 *NKJV***

The two issues — awareness and eternal life — became the source of Satan's temptation: "You will not surely die...and you will be like God..." (Genesis 3:4,5 *NKJV*). Eve, being the first tempted, ate and then offered the fruit to Adam. When the judgment of God came, man was driven from the Garden, and communion and fellowship with God was broken.

That very seed — that rebellious fist already closed against God which rises up in the heart of man — is like a microcosm of that rebellion pictured in Psalm 2. It's in all of our hearts — even in the hearts of believers. "Why can't I do this?" or, "If I want to do that, why can't I do it?"

The whole opposition to moral law, the whole situational ethic we're so deeply involved in today, comes out of man's desire not to be told there is a moral responsibility and a moral law. We must try to understand clearly this picture which shows the seething rebellion of man against the purposes of God.

We also know from Acts 4 that early believers in Jesus Christ saw the truth of Psalm 2 as specifically the rebellion which man would have against Christ. The early believers had begun to fervently witness about Jesus, who had been crucified, buried, and resurrected, and after 40 days had ascended to the Father.

They were bearing witness, believing it to be the greatest news in the world. They were telling people that God loved the world enough to send His only Son! What a wonderful message! The word that God wants to reconcile the world unto Himself through the righteousness of His Son, through the offering of His Son, ought to be banner headlines!

For their trouble, however, these early Christians were stoned. Instead of being accepted, they were persecuted and thrown into prison. When they came together in the midst of that opposition, they prayed from Psalm 2, "Lord, you wrote it through the mouth of your servant David. You said the nations would rage against the holy child Jesus, and so they have." (See Acts 4.)

And the Early Church said, based on Acts 4:24-30, "On the basis of our understanding of truth, there's something in the heart of man that rebels against the truth; and, Father, we pray that You'll give us boldness to speak the Word with truth, and not have fear in our hearts" (author's paraphrase).

In spite of the Early Church's understanding and use of Psalm 2, there is yet a literal fulfillment to be seen. Of course, nations and individuals have always raged against God and righteousness. The literal Hebrew military term here, when it says they "set" or "assembled" themselves, means "to gather together military forces" or "to muster an army." Here are the princes and the nations of the world mustering an armed force against God. And that hasn't happened yet!

Obviously, there has been a restraining force in this world. I know this world is in rebellion. I understand we are in the midst of a civilization that is in moral bankruptcy. But there is *a restraining force* in the world. The apostle Paul, in Second Thessalonians 2:7 *(NKJV)*, speaks about this power when he writes, "...He who now restrains will do so until He is taken out of the way."

I believe this verse is referring to the Holy Spirit, who in this age reveals Jesus Christ. Others see this as a reference to the Church. But the impact is the same. There is in this world a restraining force, the power of the Spirit at work through the Church, His Body, which is holding back evil like a divine "dike" against the flood of immorality, filth, and rebellion against God.

However, one day the plug will be pulled! The restrainer will be taken out of the world, and when He is gone, all destruction will break loose upon this world. The Book of Revelation tells us exactly what it will be like.

Everyone today is talking about the need for a world ruler or "new order." Many people are looking up old prophecies. Everywhere there is a sense of a divine drumbeat.

Psalm 2 declares that nations of the world will assemble in a united muster — a rebellious assemblage of material and spiritual power against God. The world alliance will meet God in a battle the world knows as much about as the

Church. Its name is used by literary sources and in newspapers. It is the name *Armageddon*.

Armageddon is an interesting word. The Hebrew *ar* or *har* simply means mountain or mound, and *megiddo* is the name of a mount that overlooks the Valley of Jehoshaphat in Israel. Here, says God's Word (Matthew 24 and Revelation 19), these forces assembled by the world in a final great act of rebellion will gather against God.

Into this conflict Jesus Christ Himself will ride forth on a white horse, with His saints following, as we see from Revelation 19:19 *(NKJV):*

And I saw the beast, the kings of the earth, and their armies, gathered together to make war against Him who sat on the horse and against His army.

This battle, which shall take place in this valley, shall be a terrible catastrophe. The blood shall splash to the horses' bridles for an area 200 miles long, and that entire Valley of Jehoshaphat shall be filled with blood and death. This must mean the farthest extension of the Rift Valley to Elat on the Red Sea.

There is, then, in this Psalm a marvelous, prophetic view which comes from the general topic of man's rebellion all the way through the specific application of a battle which is yet to take place.

But know as we study this Psalm that from beginning to end, this spirit of rebellion to divine purpose and placement is an issue for each of us. We may not arm ourselves literally against God, but the spirit of rebellion is as much an issue of our life as morning coffee or a stroll in the park.

What is God going to be doing once all these things are happening down on Earth? I am told that the Hebrew here changes its beat or pentameter in the following lines. The four lines beginning with verse 4 become a thundering declaration. The beat of the words, the poetry, plus the positioning of the words change as the psalmist shouts:

He who sits in the heavens shall laugh; the Lord shall hold them in derision.

Psalm 2:4 *NKJV*

What a contrast! Mankind on Earth is hot with hatred, flushed with defiant self-confidence, and busy with plots. The rebellion is coming together, and the rebels, like swarming ants, are trying to take the hill.

But in heaven God isn't even stirring! There is total solemnity and lack of disturbance there. It's easy to have an idea that heaven is preoccupied. God is calling in the scouts, getting the war planners together, and saying, "We've got to do something!"

No, God *already* has the victory. He's just waiting His moment. God laughs. He has them in derision. I know those are human concepts — anthropomorphisms — which means to put human emotions onto God so we can understand Him better. However that is, God is at rest.

Finally He speaks: "Yet I have set My King on My holy hill of Zion" (Palm 2:6). Where is that? What is God saying? We could paraphrase, "My eternal purposes have been declared. I am not rushing about looking for a solution. While the world is rebelling, I have declared the place from which the answer will come. I have spoken the means by which the answer will come. It is set. It is established. Nothing will change. Everything is under control. I have set my King on the holy hill of Zion."

In the next verse, the Lord Jesus Christ Himself speaks. It is the king's declaration. The Father has spoken, "I will send a King. I will establish a King." The Son now speaks, "I will declare the decree: The Lord hath said to Me...."

This word "decree" is interesting. Jesus is the speaker now. When the Messiah comes, He will, in effect, say, "I have received the decree of God, and I declare it."

God isn't secretive. He doesn't do anything in a corner. Nor is God choosing some and rejecting others. There isn't some kind of secret formula.

The world's religions all talk about mysteries and the necessity for certain special keys to unlock their secrets. Of course, you must join an inner circle to understand this so-called "mystery." The Bible, however, is as open right now for the person who has never opened it and knows nothing whatsoever about God as it is to the person who has spent a lifetime examining it.

Jesus declares, as the Messiah, "I have received a decree: and I will declare it." Jesus continually said as He walked this Earth that He was to say what the Father told Him to say; that He did what the Father told Him to do.

Can that actually be true of us? You see, the relationship with God is a family one, and that's a marvelous thing. Christians often talk about being servants of Jesus Christ, and, in a sense, they are. Jesus is King of kings and Lord of lords. Yet the relationship we enter into by faith is a family relationship.

He, the Son of God, having received the decree, declares it in His own life. Walking the shores of this life, He heals the sick, unstops deaf ears, and causes the blind to see. Jesus raised the dead, gave life, and spoke truth, declaring in Himself what the will and purposes of the Father should be. Then Jesus said to us, "I want you to be my brother, my sister. I want you, by faith in My sacrifice, to become a part of the family of God."

The New Testament changes the whole order of religion! For the first time, God is to be called "Father." The writer of Romans goes even further and says in reality that the Spirit within us will cry, "Abba, Father." You probably know that in the original language, *Abba* is the most affectionate title for "Father" that was known, such as "Papa" or "Daddy."

It's a family thing that's happened because of the sacrifice of Jesus. When we speak of the inheritance of the saints, Jesus makes sure that we say it this way. The Word makes sure that we know we are heirs of the Father and joint-heirs with the Son. I love to sing a little Gospel chorus which says:

We are heirs of the Father,

We are joint-heirs with the Son.
We are children of the Kingdom,
We're a family — we are one.[8]

What a wonderful truth! All of the kingdom of God has become ours through Jesus. That which He received, He declared. Psalm 2 further declares that believers might ask and receive the inheritance of the world.

That which continues in rebellion receives a rod of judgment which would break the remaining rebellion of the world so it would look like a piece of pottery, smashed by an iron rod.

There is this perfect balance of the revelation of God. On one side is God's declaration of Sonship, family, and mercy. But on the other side is a rebellion smashed like pottery onto which a truckload of iron has dropped.

Perhaps no verse in the Old Testament is more important to believers than Psalm 2:8 *(NKJV):* "Ask of Me, and I will give *You*...." Notice that the word "You" is in italics. Whenever that happens in a translation, it simply means that the word is not in the original manuscript.

Reading on, you will find the same thing with the phrase "...the nations for Your inheritance, and the ends of the earth for Your possession." Again, neither of the words "for" are in the manuscripts. It actually should read this way: "Ask of Me, and I will give You Your inheritance, which is the nations." Thus, the Father is saying to Jesus, "You will ask, and I will give You that which is Your inheritance."

This is not a request for something that has not already been assured. The guarantee has already been made. Paul, writing to the Philippians, said:

that at the name of Jesus every knee should bow...

and that every tongue should confess that Jesus Christ is Lord, to the glory of God the Father.

Philippians 2:10,11 *NKJV*

We are all going to be a part of that! A man can rebel against God, religion, and Christians. He can get uptight with preachers and even have them broiled or sauteed, but the simple truth is that everyone will be on one side or the other.

One choice is to be a person who says, by his own will, "Jesus, I receive You as Lord and believe in Your Saviorhood. I repent of my sin and take You into my life voluntarily to be the Lord of my life."

The alterative is to be a part of the total world inheritance which will bow a bow of *obeisance;* the bow of a slave. Then they will say, "You are right — You *are* Lord. My way of rebellion was useless. You are the King and Lord of creation. And when it came time, You asked of the Father, and He gave You that which was Your inheritance, which is the kingdoms of this world."

The Bible ends with a simple statement; a declaration that the kingdoms of this world have become the kingdoms of our God and of His Christ. We know the end of the story! There is no doubt about it.

You may look at this seething world and think there is a great battle going on. The outcome appears to be in question. But when you look at it from God's prospect, it is just a futile endeavor of rebellion. It is a fight that is already finished. The kingdoms of this world have become the kingdoms of our God and of His Christ!

I want you to see that when God is finally ready to put an end to this rebellion, it is just like smashing pieces of pottery.

On a recent trip to Israel, our tour group became very familiar with the word "potsherds." No, it's not a swear word! Potsherds are the little pieces of broken pottery that archaeology seems to live by. A major archaeological find will include thousands of pieces of these potsherds.

There are people who spend their whole professional lives putting such potsherds back together. Generally, when you see a lovely ancient vase, urn, plate, or similar object in a museum, you are not seeing something which was found in that condition. It was actually pieced back together from many pieces of broken potsherds.

Just a little piece of pottery — that's what God says the rebellion of the world will be at the end: like a piece of iron dropping on a piece of pottery! The Word even says that God will use *only* His Word, and that will be enough. His Word will finish it all!

Finally, the psalmist ends with a personal word in this prophecy. "Now therefore," he writes, or on the basis of this, "be wise, O kings; be instructed, you judges of the earth." And what is the conclusion?

Serve the Lord with fear, and rejoice with trembling.

Kiss the Son, lest He be angry, and you perish in the way, when his wrath is kindled but a little. Blessed are all those who put their trust in Him.

Psalm 2:10-12 *NKJV*

We have now reviewed the second Psalm. There are many personal implications in its words. Remember, we are not studying these Psalms simply for great expositional truths, but as the practical experience of a man's life trying to know God and let God be known in his life. Why?

For me, the first word of Psalm 2 is so important. That word "why" is reflected in a believer's life, and it is reflected from Psalm to Psalm throughout this book. It is the cry of any man or woman of God who says, "How can this be? How can the unrighteous prosper and the righteous suffer?"

The cry is eternal in the heart, and we all identify with it. Why hasn't God shut down the world? Why is there a tomorrow when men continue to live in their rebellion and unrighteousness? The writer is honest with his question so God can be specific with an answer. That's a lesson for all of us.

I also love to remember how this Psalm encouraged the Early Christian Church in one of its greatest moments of persecution, when the Early Church was being so oppressed they must have wondered if they had chosen the right thing.

All society seemed to be turned against their simple proclamation that Jesus was Lord. But when they went to this Psalm, they were encouraged. Then they could pray God's words back to Him:

"God, You spoke through Your prophets that the nations seem absolutely, adamantly opposed to any revelation of truth that you give them. They have opposed Your holy child Jesus. Now God, strengthen our hearts so we can proclaim the Word boldly."

I see in this Psalm a word of peace to the believer. Yes, there is going to be opposition, and it will sometimes rage as a mighty, stormy sea about you with ferment and foam. You may even think everything is lost. Quietly, the Holy Spirit brings a word of encouragement concerning God's control from this very Psalm: "Blessed are all those who put their trust in Him."

In our laboratory of life, we must remind ourselves of another principle found in this Psalm. Four times the small phrase "the Lord" is used in Psalm 2. The rebellion is against *the Lord,* and it is *the Lord* who shall have them in derision. Do you know what the word means in the original?

Most manuscripts have the word *Adonai* for *the Lord,* although a small number have *Jehovah* or even *Elohim. Adonai* is a word meaning "ruler of the world," a word used for magistrates. You may also interpret *Lord* as, "He is my Stay, my Sustainer, my Pillar. He is the One upon whom I lean."

That is the alternative question, you see. We can't always make sense out of what is happening in this world. We can't understand why our loved one lies in a hospital bed, perhaps dying from cancer or the like, even when he or she is a dear saint of God.

We can't understand why God allows someone who is loved and needed by family and friends to go through that situation. I have personally faced that quandary before, as you have. My sister, at 45 years of age, died of cancer. I will not understand the ultimate things of that situation in this lifetime.

What is happening in all the diversity of world affairs? The psalmist simply points us to a central truth and says, "I know the Word. I know Adonai is the strength and stability of my life. I don't understand why He lets things go as He does. I don't understand why His timing isn't my timing. I don't understand the circumstances that surround me, but He is still the Lord."

My friend, it is not for nothing that in order to be a believer you must confess with your mouth that Jesus Christ is *Lord!* There's no hope for a new life just by believing in the cross. The devils believe and tremble, according to James 2:19. The hope for new life comes when He, who is Savior, becomes *Lord.* Then the strength and central purpose of your life becomes that pillar, and the raging sands and seas of this life cannot destroy Him.

It is imperative that we live out our days recognizing that our time and our schedule is not necessarily the Lord's. Psalm 2:5 uses the all-important word "then" or "again." The original language suggests "after a time" or "presently."

The entire passage describes rebellion and activity on Earth, with God maintaining calm in heaven. God seems somewhat uninvolved except for a laugh or two! But then He speaks. After a specific time He takes action.

The writer to the Ephesians says, "that in the dispensation of the fullness of the times He might gather together in one all things in Christ..." (Ephesians 1:10 *NKJV*).

Don't try to set dates and run away from practical involvement in this world. Be very cautious about so-called personal prophecy which directs your life in unusual directions. There are always repeatable cycles of these things in the Church's history. Perhaps the Church hasn't had 2000 years of history at all, but rather 40 years of history repeated 50 times!

Doesn't it seem like you have been through some of these cycles before? If God seems to be inactive now against unrighteousness, He will stand with the hot, blazing anger of fury on His face.

God is going to take action against the unrighteousness of this world, and that little word "then" in verse 5 is a reminder that it is going to happen. We have read the last chapter of the book, and we know who wins. It's the Lord!

Perhaps *place* is as much a problem as *time*. Where should we focus our life — on what cause or purpose? Psalm 2 calls our attention to Zion. God says, "Don't worry. I've set My King on My holy hill of Zion."

Geographically, Zion is the mountainous hill area in present-day Jerusalem. It was first used, as far as history is concerned, by a little group of people called the Jebusites. One of their kings, Melchizedek, is prominently named in the New Testament Book of Hebrews. We don't know much about those Jebusites, but they obviously had some manner of spiritual truth. Eventually, David conquered the Jebusites and purchased this very Mount Zion. In the early years of his kingship, David brought the Ark of the Covenant from the property of Abinadab and put the ark on Mount Zion. That became a precedent. It was the beginning of the hope that God would eventually allow a temple to be built there.

Psalm 2 goes even further, saying that God would put His King on Zion. That, of course, spoke of the Messiah. Did you ever wonder what the word "Zion" means? I am told it implies "a distant view." The Church, which is the Zion of God, has always been a people who had a distant view. There can be little doubt about that.

The world today, with its huge buildings, great armies, and military power, seems to be winning the power. True Christianity seems but a microcosm. But God says, "I have set My King on the holy hill of Zion." It's in that distant view — it's with that distant hope — that the Church can win. We must see *ahead* of the temporary and the now; beyond the passing and the transient we must learn to see the eternal.

Our laboratory of life is meant to be an experience of worship. It is godly reverence, yet rejoicing with great joy. Psalm 2:11 shows us that perfect mixture. This is how we truly come to know God.

The whole basis of walking the Christian life is about balance. There is great danger in imbalance. For example, our teaching in the area of grace can end up with a kind of licentiousness and "cheap grace," which is a *disgrace!*

On the other hand, a legalism and a bondage of Christian law will neither exalt the Lord nor draw attention to Jesus. There must be a perfect balance. The man who doesn't walk in the ways of the ungodly delights in the Lord and is blessed of the Lord.

There is a rod *and* a staff in the hands of the Good Shepherd. In this Psalm, the psalmist says, "On the basis of all these things being true, serve or worship the Lord with godly reverence and fear, yet rejoice in Him with all joy and trembling." That's the combination which produces balance and true worship.

Psalm 2 closes with the strangest admonition: "Kiss the Son, lest He be angry, and you perish in the way..." (verse 12). The original manuscript suggests, "lest the way becomes closed to you."

The phrase "kiss the Son" may seem like a strange way for a writer to close what is doubtlessly one of the great philosophical and religious passages of the world. It seems strange for a man who has wrestled with rebellion and unrighteousness and who has had a vision from his own day entirely through the Millennium, which will end this world. "Kiss the Son" seems so simple and strange, yet it is filled with truth.

The Middle Eastern world knew the kiss primarily as an act of worship and adoration. It was a part of every worship form or system, including that of Jehovah. To "kiss the Son" is to worship Him.

71

Second, the kiss was an imperative act of obeisance and homage. It was made to a king or a ruler. That seems to be its primary use in this passage. The concept seems to be, "Do obeisance to Him and accept His Lordship, or His wrath will be kindled."

To refuse to kiss the Son would be the great insult of refusing to bow in the presence of royalty. Kiss the Son. Do obedience and obeisance to the Son. Pay homage to Him. Receive the Son as Lord, lest His anger be kindled against you.

Now let us divide the Middle Eastern understanding entirely from our own. Then, as now, the kiss is one of affection and love of communion and relationship. This Psalm has taken us through the whole gamut of human history: the seething rebellion of a world that will not have God's law; the infinite patience of God, sitting while the raging storm goes on below; and finally acting by speaking the Word and setting His King upon the holy hill of Zion.

The very decree of the Messiah Himself in verse 7 — "I will declare the decree: The Lord has said to Me, You are My Son, today I have begotten You" — is both a word of peace and a word of crushing.

Finally, the psalmist, as an impassioned presenter of truth, cries out, "Be wise...be instructed...Serve the Lord...Kiss the Son, lest He be angry, and you perish in the way [or the way be closed to you]..." (Psalm 2:10-12).

Here is the tragedy. The way of God gets closed to us in many ways: hardness of heart, rejection of truth, rebellion against God, the deceitfulness of sin, the craftiness of men, and the bitterness, intolerance, and frustration of life experience. These are all ways our way gets closed. These are avalanches of human events which close the one passage through the mountain which leads to peace.

Let us hear this psalmist in the deepest part of our understanding. First, to unbelievers the psalmist is writing, *"Kiss the Son"* now before God turns from patience to the fury of His anger to destroy a rebellious world system. Receive Jesus Christ, the Messiah, *now* as your personal Lord and Savior. Do obeisance to Him *now*, lest the way be closed.

Jesus taught in Luke 11 that there are many ways in which people meet their end. Some people are killed by tragic accidents. The tower of Siloam fell and killed 18 Jews. Jesus asked, "Do you think that they were worse sinners than all other men who dwelt in Jerusalem?" (Luke 13:4 *NKJV*). They simply died. It was the end of the way for them.

Jesus also told of a group of Galileans whose blood Pilate had mingled with the sacrifices (Luke 13:1,2). "Do you suppose that these Galileans were worse sinners than all other Galileans, because they suffered such things?"He asked. Here, circumstances and the will of men were involved, but the issue is the same. There is a closure which will come to each person's life. There is a time when there is no longer an open door. Kiss the Son *now*.

We have seen that the concept ending Psalm 2 is not only Lordship or obedience; it is also worship. The primary direction of the psalmist does seem to be evangelistic, but I would argue that this is not his *entire* direction.

Psalm 2 presents a dilemma of delay in believers' expectations as well: a seemingly silent God in a raucous and rebellious world. Do believers LIVE their lives sometimes angry, offended, and out of vital fellowship and open worship with their Lord? The answer is, all too often, *yes.*

To "kiss the Son" is to accept His whole purpose toward our lives as good. Not everything in this fallen world has been His direction, but His *grace* has been in everything.

A Christian must always watch for the mud and avalanches which close the way to intimate, joyous worship and relationship with King Jesus.

[1]Harold A. Bosley, *Sermons on the Psalms*, Harper and Brothers, New York.

[2]Arthur Fletcher, as quoted by Harold A. Bosley, op. cit., p. 40.

[3]John Henry Nash.

[4]Clare Boothe Luce, article in *Life* magazine.

[5]Niels C. Nielsen Jr., *Solzhenitsyn's Religion.* Thomas Nelson, Nashville.

[6]*The Collected Poems of A. E. Housman.* Henry Holt and Company, Inc., 1940.

[7]Yalkut Shinoni, as quoted by Arno C. Gaebelein in *The Book of Psalms*, Van Kampen Press, 1939.

[8]*We Are Family*, Jimmy and Carol Owens, Lexicon Music, 1974.

The Laboratory of Life

SECTION 3

The Time In Between:
Biblical Kairos in Our Lives

(Psalms 3 Through 7)

And tho' this world with devils filled
Should threaten to undo us;
We will not fear for God hath willed
His truth to triumph through us.
      —Martin Luther
        "A Mighty Fortress Is
        Our God"

If the rest of scripture may be called the speech of the Spirit of God to man, this book [the Psalms] *is the answer of the Spirit of God in man.*[1]
> —Alexander Maclaren

$\mathscr{P}$SALM $\mathcal{3}$

Lord, how they have increased that trouble me! Many are they who rise up against me.

Many are they who say of me, "There is no help for him in God."

But You, O Lord, are a shield for me, my glory and the one who lifts up my head.

I cried to the Lord with my voice, and He heard me from His holy hill.

I lay down and slept; I awoke, for the Lord sustained me.

I will not be afraid of ten thousands of people, who have set themselves against me all around.

Arise, O Lord; save me, O my God! For You have struck all my enemies on the cheekbone; You have broken the teeth of the ungodly.

Salvation belongs to the Lord. Your blessing is upon Your people.

NKJV

CHAPTER 7

The Time In Between

(Psalms 3 Through 7)

*F*rom the seventh Psalm we read:

O Lord my God, in thee do I put my trust: save me from all them that persecute me, and deliver me:

Lest he tear my soul like a lion, rending it in pieces, while there is none to deliver...

I will praise the Lord according to his righteousness: and will sing praise to the name of the Lord most high.

Psalm 7:1,2,17

Everyone who attempts to walk faithfully and honestly before God is aware of the difficult moment between revelation and accomplishment; between promise and fulfillment; between faith and victory.

It is that monstrously difficult waiting period in which we must battle between the Word of God to us versus the actual circumstances. It is often a "dark moment" of our soul. I believe that is in essence the story of the next five Psalms.

They are gigantic Psalms by their personal application, if not in number of words. These Psalms describe such a *time in between* — a time so common to everyone in the laboratory of life. I desire that our simple introduction to this material may quicken the Word of God to you, becoming letters of life.

When I think of such a time in life, I think about our Lord Jesus Christ, who, on the blackest night of human history, walked out of Jerusalem and crossed the little brook of

79

Kidron, going down into the valley. Then He began to walk up the Mount of Olives to a place called "the oil press" or Gethsemane. Here the Messiah, the Son of God, the God-King, having come to this Earth, agonized with His rejection.

You will recall that the second Psalm became precious to the Early Christian Church when they were persecuted in the first century. Acts 4 says they lifted up their voices to God with one accord and repeated the words of David concerning the rebellion of the Earth — peoples and leaders against the King Messiah.

Actually, Psalm 2 is the first *Messianic* Psalm. It is about Jesus being rejected: the rejection of God's Anointed and how that rejection eventually would accelerate. We know that rejection of God's truth, a rejection which has been in every age, will accelerate until at the end of the age, which we are facing now, the kings of this Earth will actually gather together militarily against God!

Psalm 2, you will remember, is a prophetic statement about that great conflagration where God, through Christ and the host of heaven, will fight the world powers under the Antichrist at the battle of Armageddon. We know how it is going to end!

If we jump ahead a bit, we should briefly note the second great Messianic Psalm in the Old Testament: Psalm 8. *Here, the opposite is true.* Here, He who is the Son of man will have *all* things put under His feet. Psalm 8 is the glorious prophecy of the ultimate victory of Christ. It is the realization of what Paul wrote in Philippians 2:10 and 11 *(NKJV):*

> that at the name of Jesus every knee should bow, of those in heaven, and of those on earth, and of those under the earth,
>
> and that every tongue should confess that Jesus Christ is Lord, to the glory of God the Father.

Psalm 8 is shouting territory!

But you must see with me that Psalms 3 through 7 are the *in between time.* They mark the time between the Messiah's coming and being rejected and His eventual Second Coming, in which He will indeed be King of kings and Lord of lords. Then, as we believe, the kingdoms of this world will become the kingdoms of our God and of His Christ.

There are five Psalms between the cross and the crown. Specifically, the Holy Spirit wrote in Hebrews 2:8:

You have put all things in subjection under his feet. For in that He put all in subjection under him, He left nothing that is not put under him.

That's the time in between. Faith says Psalm 8 is already true. Faith says Jesus is already King of kings and Lord of lords, and every knee shall bow and every tongue confess Him Lord to the glory of God the Father. But in reality we do not yet see these things as true. We are in the time in between.

That's why I believe these Psalms belong together. They form a bridge which leads from one great Messianic Psalm (Psalm 2) to the other great Messianic Psalm (Psalm 8). This bridge is specifically built on the following four bases of interpretation, any one of which could consume a book itself.

First, these Psalms obviously have a historical application to David.

Second, they specifically are the words and prayers which Israel both has and will pray in her tribulation when she is being troubled by those who will do all in their power to destroy what is left of God's Chosen People.

Third, many of the words which we study in these five Psalms were spoken out of Jesus' mouth during some of His own times of testing; during His own time in between.

Fourth, these five Psalms speak volumes of wisdom concerning the Church and each of us individually during such periods of our own life.

If Psalms 3 through 7 are like a bridge, the river which flows under that bridge is *the river of time*. The Bible says, "My times are in thy hand." And Paul wrote to the Ephesians:

...in the dispensation of the fullness of the times He might gather together in one all things in Christ, both which are in heaven and which are on earth — in Him.

Ephesians 1:10 *NKJV*

So you see, time is a steward in our lives, and one such time is the time in between — in between the word and the fulfillment — in between the faith and the victory — in between the promise and its realization.

It would be helpful to examine what we can know of the historical background of these five Psalms. The inscription of Psalm 3 was possibly written by the original writer — David, in this instance.

It reads, "A Psalm of David, when he fled from Absalom his son." I almost want to weep on reading that line without even going into the rest of the story. It is emotionally told in Second Samuel chapters 15 through 18. Psalm 4 is believed by almost all scholars to be in that same time period, the Absalomic rebellion.

If we look ahead to Psalm 7, the last of these five Psalms, we see that this Psalm is called a "Shiggaion of David" in most older translations. *Shiggaion* is an interesting word which means "a wail or a cry out loud." It also refers to a variable experience; a cry which is a kind of erratic, out-loud kind of thing.

This is a special kind of Psalm. We all feel like crying out loud sometimes, but David's experience at this point was during a specific moment. Notice the inscription of Psalm 7: "A *Shiggaion* of David, which he sang unto the Lord, concerning the words of Cush the Benjamite."

Who is Cush? There are many theories concerning this, and we need not trouble ourselves with them at this point. The most obvious explanation is that in Psalm 7 David is writing about the foul-mouthed descendant of Saul whose name was Shimei.

It was Shimei who cursed and stoned David as he fled in disgrace before his son Absalom (2 Samuel 16:5-13). If we know that Psalms 3 and 4 apply to that incident before Absalom, and we presume that Psalm 7 was also written during the experience, I would like to suggest that all five of these Psalms *probably* apply to that same historical event.

Here is David fleeing from his son! I know to some scholars this is an oversimplification. I also know we can't be sure, because we don't know about the exact time and period. But this I know from these five Psalms: They all relate to that kind of a circumstance. There is no reason not to believe they were written in this particular period of David's life.

Can you see now that these five Psalms represent the greatest moment of *time in between* in the life of David? There were many such times for David. There was the time after he was anointed king; then all those years while Saul, that one from whom the Spirit of God had departed, chased him from pillar to post.

Yet that was not the roughest time for David. That was not his greatest time in between. The greatest — and surely in his heart the longest — moment of David's spiritual experience was this episode of fleeing before his son Absalom.

Let me briefly retell that story. In many ways it is the saddest, most pathetic, and most pathos-filled incident in the Bible. It must begin with David's adultery with Bathsheba and end with David crying at the body of his son, "O Absalom, my son, my son!" David's sin had not simply been adultery. God, through the prophet Nathan, reveals the sin to include the whole covetousness that was a part of David's nature.

He had to have the best, even though it was someone else's possession. The parable Nathan spoke to David concerning that sin was about a man who had only one lamb. The wealthy neighbor, who had many lambs on every hillside, insisted on taking the one lamb from the man who had only one and killing it to feed his guests. That was how God saw David's sin; not specifically the adultery, as heinous as that was in itself, but the *motivation* of David's heart.

Remember when Nathan exposed that sin to David, God spoke these words through the prophet: "Behold, I will raise up evil against you out of your own house" (2 Samuel 12:11). And that specific word from God to David became a foundation for many of David's most difficult experiences; yet, at the same time, his greatest ultimate victories.

Did it happen? Some scholars list 20 ways in which David paid for that sin. We must establish this truth in our hearts: *A covenant person who has a relationship with God cannot sin and escape.* Certainly, a covenant person does not lose his *relationship* with God when he sins, but he loses his *fellowship* and then pays in his life.

The Bible says, "Whatsoever a man sows, that will he also reap. For he who sows to his flesh will of the flesh reap corruption..." (Galatians 6:7,8). Remember that David hid the sin by the unthinkable murder of his close associate, Captain Uriah, the husband of Bathsheba. What a terrible act that was! The consequences were equally awful. First, the child conceived in this sin died, although David prayed and fasted.

Then, in his own house, one of David's sons, Amnon, looked upon his 15-year-old half-sister, Tamar, and lusted after her. He devised a scheme whereby she was tricked into his quarters. There Amnon raped her and ultimately thrust her out in rejection.

Tamar's brother Absalom, born of the same mother, was a handsome young son of David. Absalom, in vengeance, came upon his unrighteous brother who had committed this atrocious act against his sister and killed him. For that he was banished from David's sight and the kingdom and lived in exile for three or four years. Finally in a merciful act David brought Absalom out of banishment but never (at least in scriptural record) totally reconciled the son to himself.

The years of banishment had festered in Absalom's heart like a burning sore. He came back into the kingdom with one purpose in mind: to take it away from his father! We are told that he was brilliant as well as handsome.

One of his clever strategies was to take 50 young friends who were excellent charioteers and station them at strategic points so whenever anyone came to Jerusalem to get counsel from the king, these young men would stop them and send them to Absalom instead.

Absalom would then say, "It's true. You have a pitiful case. If only we had a better king. If *I* were king, I would know

how righteous your cause is. If *I* were king, I'd see to it that..."
and so forth. It sounds like a political campaign, doesn't it?

The Bible records that Absalom, after having done that,
would reach out and embrace the person to himself and kiss
him. He did this for a period of several years, making intimate friends of all these people coming to the king for advice.
Thus, the hearts of the people of Israel began to wax warm
toward Absalom.

Finally, under the ruse of having a vow-worship, Absalom asked his father for the privilege of going to Hebron.
Hebron, of course, was where David had been crowned king.
The message was soon sent by Absalom's young couriers
across the land: "When you hear the sound of the trumpet out
of Hebron, know that Absalom is made king." And so it was.

Counselors came to David and said, "Absalom has been
proclaimed king, and all of Israel has gone after him!" Perhaps the worst news of all was that David's closest friend and
counselor, and perhaps the greatest spiritual leader in the
kingdom, Ahithophel, also fled to Absalom. The Bible says
that when this man gave advice, it was as though the word of
God was spoken directly (2 Samuel 16:23). He was a spiritual
man and an intimate friend of David.

When David heard that Ahithophel had betrayed him,
he said to his couriers, "Gather up the household and let us
flee." One of the most pitiful views a reader can find in the
Bible is found in Second Samuel 16.

David, wearing a simple houserobe, with nothing on his
feet, trudged in haste across the brook Kidron and up the
Mount of Olives with 600 household servants. What a vision!
As this bedraggled company of Israel's spiritually ordained
leadership made their way up the Mount of Olives, along
came Shimei, a descendant of former King Saul.

He had been harboring resentment against the house of
David from the day David had become king. This was his
chance for vengeance! He cursed the king, spat on him —
and even stoned him!

David's nephew asked for permission to kill Shimei. But David said, "No, do not defend me." When they reached the top of the Mount of Olives, the Bible records that David offered a worship offering to God. His followers had brought the Ark of the Covenant with them, but David commanded that it be sent back to Jerusalem. "If God wills, I will come back to the ark, but the ark has no right to go with me," he said. So he trudged on.

Can you imagine that scene! Do you know how many people had followed Absalom? So many had followed him that 20,000 fell in battle in one day!

The night Absalom came into Jerusalem and discovered that King David had fled, Ahithophel had given him the advice, "Take 12,000 and chase after David, and we will conquer him." Indeed, they would have, but God had placed another man, whose name was Hushai, to counsel Absalom, and Hushai's heart was true to David. Therefore, Hushai purposely counseled Absalom wrongly, and he did not pursue David.

Of course, the story turned at this point. You already know this. That's the advantage of hindsight. But this, I believe, is the story out of which these five Psalms came into existence. This is the great *time in between* for David — a moment between promise and fulfillment — a dark moment which we could call David's Gethsemane. How ironic that Jesus would take the identical route to His Gethsemane that David had used when he fled Jerusalem.

Do not make the mistake of viewing these Psalms as a simple historical view of David. This is a stone on which a bridge is built applicable to us all. The truths apply as strongly to Christ and Israel, each with their rejection, but also in a uniquely personal way to us.

Our laboratory of life will include this basic experience in one way or another. May we learn vicariously from the costly, vulnerable sharing of this truth with us!

O, yet we trust that somehow good
Will be the final goal of ill,

That nothing walks with aimless feet;
That not one life shall be destroy'd,
Or cast as rubbish to the void
When God hath made the pile complete;

I can but trust that good shall fall
At last — far off — at last, to all...
                      —Tennyson, "In Memoriam,"
                          Poem, 1850

CHAPTER 8

Lessons To Be Learned From Waiting

*T*he Psalms are real songs from life. They describe godly but often confused believers living out the details of a realistic experience. Their individual experiences are like laboratory experiments carefully annotated for the benefit of others.

We are looking at five Psalms together — Psalms 3 through 7 — and they are a unique entity. They comprise, I believe, a description of a common Christian dilemma, the time in between promise and fulfillment, call and covenant, and faith and ultimate victory. As such, these Psalms are some of the richest ground for a believer's consideration.

There are a few of us who do not identify personally. While teaching some of these truths in my church, a man from the congregation came into my office with a personal report. "I'm in the divine experiment, all right," he said, "but somebody has turned up the Bunsen burner!" This is one of the common happenings in a laboratory.

Now let's review briefly. Psalm 2 is the first great Messianic Psalm in the Book of Psalms. It is clearly about the character of Christ as well as being a challenge to each of us. Psalm 8, similarly, is the second great Messianic Psalm concerning Christ's ultimate victory. The interesting series of five Psalms we are now studying is like a bridge between these two important Psalms.

In Psalm 2, the rejection of God's Anointed is depicted. He will come, it says, and there will be rebellion against Him; a rebellion that will increase until it ultimately will be a worldwide war against God. This war has not yet taken place, but when it does, all the iniquity of the world will marshal its forces against God and His truth.

The eighth Psalm, on the other hand, declares that all things will be put under the feet of Jesus Christ. It is the glorious prophecy of an ultimate victory for the Christ. It concerns Christ's Second Coming and the time He will become Lord of the world.

Spanning these historical moments is what we have called the time in between. Hebrews 2:8 *(NKJV)* describes it by saying, "...But now we do not yet see all things put under him." Psalm 8 is not yet true, and we are living in this moment before fulfillment. These five Psalms are a bridge between that faith and fulfillment and between that promise and completion!

We have already noted the historical basis of these Psalms. Although all scholars would not agree, we have assigned these five Psalms basically to one period. As we have seen, the handwritten instructions for the third and seventh Psalms identify them with the period of Absalom's rebellion. You will discover that the three others belonged either to that period directly or certainly to that kind of circumstance.

These five Psalms represented a time in between for David — an experience of life between God's promises to him and their fulfillment. These were the dark moments of David's soul, when he ultimately fled with a small band of men down the Kidron Valley, driven from his throne by his son Absalom and, what the scripture says, "all the people"! The host of Israel had gone after the rebel, and David, the king, had to flee with his band of loyalists. The Bunsen burner was indeed hot for David!

Clearly, as is often true in the Psalms, there are other implications. The Messiah, as we have seen, is clearly referred to here. Jesus Christ came and was rejected. Certainly not every knee is bowing today to Jesus Christ; nor is every tongue confessing Him as Lord of lords! He is still being rejected, but we know He will come again in power and great glory.

These Psalms also represent that difficult time in between, when the Church, that great mystery of Scripture, is being released and fulfilled.

And, of course, Israel is included in this period. Without being divisive over the issue of prophecy, I believe these five Psalms will be a literal prayer of Israel in her moment of torment in future tribulation.

I also believe that Jesus Christ will come the second time — first for the Church, which will rise to meet Him in the air; and then with the Church He shall come in judgment against the nations at the battle of Armageddon.

Events in that period of time will include a speeded-up presentation of the Gospel, including horrible persecution against the Gospel witnesses. The persecution of Jerusalem and the Jews shall become intense.

I believe that this time will end in the 200-mile-long Valley of Jehoshaphat, and that it will be filled with blood splashing to the horses' bridles. It will be in those moments that Israel will pray some of these kingdom prayers in the Psalms.

We often have trouble with some of these so-called imprecatory prayers, such as, "Lord, break their jawbones," "Lord, break their teeth," and so forth. Some Christians reading these verses feel like the little girl who thought they were written before God became a Christian! Nevertheless, they are prayers which will be a part of that specific time and era.

The Book of Revelation tells us that the Tribulation saints who die in that awful bloodshed will be praying, "Lord, how long until You avenge us of our blood?" Revenge is not a Christian prayer; these are kingdom prayers prayed during this era.

We have now traced these three applications: *historical,* in reference to David; *Messianic,* in reference to Christ; and *prophetic,* in reference to Israel, because I believe we must understand the background in its widest scale.

Applications for Contemporary Christians

But our focus in this book is upon our own Christian life. That is why I want to trace in this chapter lessons for all people who are in a time in between faith and victory. David learned these lessons, then wrote concerning them for others. They apply to us as literally as anything possibly could. Now let us look carefully at these applications.

First is an important lesson from Psalm 3. This has been called "The Morning Psalm" or "The Morning Hymn." It was written by David as he fled from his son Absalom. We took almost an entire chapter to describe that event for David as given in Second Samuel.

It was a horrible ordeal! Every doubt and fear that any believer can ever know must have been present in that experience. Yet David here describes a principle essential for every believer's peace while he or she waits in such a time in between.

Psalm 3:1,2 *(NKJV)* says:

Lord, how they have increased who trouble me! Many are they who rise up against me.

Many are they who say of me, "There is no help for him in God."

Perhaps the cruelest thing of all is when friends and loved ones, particularly in the believing community or even in the same spiritual calling, begin to turn against us. It is the bitterest of all pills to swallow and is probably the hardest of all personal experiences.

You remember that the Bible says *all* of Israel had turned against David. After his exile, Absalom stole the hearts of Israel away from his father, David. Now this great king and his little remnant fled against his greatly increased enemies. Their worst taunt against David is found in the words, "There is no help for him in God."

Some Christians strongly believe that God will always alter their circumstances. They tend to believe that they will always get well immediately when they are sick and that every disease will be healed quickly. How easy it is to think that when things are difficult, or we are suffering from privation, job loss, or misunderstanding, there should always be *instant* changes.

When these changes or interventions do not immediately appear, someone is bound to say, "Something must be wrong in that person's spiritual life. He is not being healed. She didn't get an answer to that prayer. That trial has continued for a longer period of time than normal."

Even Paul himself, the great apostle, writes in Philippians 1 about the fact that since he had been in jail four years, his own brethren were preaching the Gospel by contention, hoping to add *affliction* to his bonds! (See Philippians 1:15,16.)

And what a fine bunch of godly friends gathered around Job. Haven't you seen that same crowd before?

David said, "How they have increased who trouble me! They say of me, 'There is no help for him in God.'" What is the lesson of experience? It's very simple: God must get David down to basics. God wants David to turn away from everything else and to hope *only* in Him.

In Psalm 3:3 David cries out, "But You, O Lord, are a shield for me, my glory and the One who lifts up my head." David was saying, "It isn't the circumstance or my friends — it isn't even the fulfillment of a promise — that counts. It is *You*, God. You and You alone!

In Genesis 14, Abraham was brought to that place after a great military adventure in which he had taken 318 of his trained servants and went all the way across country to Dan, where he recaptured Lot, his nephew, and his possessions. But later, as revealed in Genesis 15, Abraham experienced a moment of great spiritual depression.

He said in essence to God, "I know I'm never going to have an heir. It's obvious You're not going to give me a son as You promised, so I'll give my inheritance to someone else." God spoke to him that night and said, "*I am your shield*, your exceedingly great reward."

 PSALM 4

*Hear me when I call, O God my righteousness! You have relieved
me when I was in distress; have mercy on me, and hear my prayer.*

*How long, O you sons of men, will you turn my glory to shame?
How long will you love worthlessness and seek falsehood?*

*But know that the Lord has set apart for Himself him who is godly;
the Lord will hear when I call to Him.*

*Be angry, and do not sin. Meditate within your heart on your bed,
and be still.*

Offer the sacrifices of righteousness, and put your trust in the Lord.

*There are many who say, "Who will show us any good?" Lord, lift
up the light of Your countenance upon us.*

*You have put gladness in my heart, more than in the season that
their grain and wine increased.*

*I will both lie down in peace, and sleep; for You alone, O Lord, make
me dwell in safety.*

NKJV

God must often remove the thing we *want* in order to give us the thing we *need*. The ultimate lesson of a time in between is that it is God *alone* — not God plus religious experience and not God plus *anything* — but God *alone!* Unfortunately, it is a relatively small group of Christians who fight their way through to that spiritual place.

Their attitude is, "God, You're my shield. My success is not found in my armies; it's not found in my couriers; it's not found in my position; it's not even found in the call You gave me or in your anointing upon me. *You* are my shield. *You* are my reward."

On the basis of that lesson, David could then say, "I lay down and slept; I awoke, for the Lord sustained me" (Psalm 3:5).

There must be a place in a relationship with God in which He will shake everything else loose. I suppose you can be a Christian and get through life and never come to this place; but you can never be a spiritual man or woman of God without coming to the moment when all the props are knocked out from under you.

Perhaps that will include friends and loved ones. Certainly it includes feelings and emotions. Then you get down to the basic substance of *just God*. The wonderful thing you discover in that moment is that *He is enough!* You don't need anything else.

George Matheson, the great songwriter, said, "It is Thee, and not Thy gifts, that I crave." There must be nothing which so pleases the heart of God as a believer who has come to the place where he can pray, "Lord, it's You I want — not your gifts, not your answers, and not all the 'goodies' — I just want You." David learned this in his time in between. Such times are always ripe for such serendipities.

Circumstances Are Meaningful

Interestingly, the fourth Psalm is often called "The Evening Hymn" — "An evening hymn with a special note to the first chair violin." That's really what it says: "To the first or chief Musician on the stringed instruments."

The issue from this Psalm for people who are in a time in between is that *the circumstances are meaningful.* Perhaps this is even harder to learn than *God is enough.*

Some people say, "If I could just look through this and see God, I'd be able to hold on." But what David is saying in Psalm 4 is you need a spiritual vision that will show you the place for the circumstance itself. You need to be able to thank God specifically for that circumstance which you are enduring.

Hear me when I call, O God of my righteousness! You have relieved me when I was in distress; have mercy on me, and hear my prayer.

Psalm 4:1 *NKJV*

The literal Hebrew says, "You have enlarged or made room for me through my persecution, through my tribulation." In other words, David is saying, "This experience which You have sent to me has been Your means to making me a greater person. You have enlarged me. You have made room for me through this tribulation."

Later in chapter 4, David says, "But know that the Lord has set apart for Himself him who is godly..." (verse 3). We might paraphrase David, "I'm exactly where I am supposed to be." Most of us are all for leaving; especially if the place is uncomfortable!

Paul, in Philippians, is writing to fellow believers after enduring four years of imprisonment. He had spent the last two years under house arrest in Rome. Paul's arms were bound to two Roman guards, one for each arm. This was the most personally debilitating and uncomfortable kind of imprisonment.

Yet Paul says in Philippians 1:17, "I am appointed for the defense of the gospel." The interesting military term Paul uses here, *keimei*, says in the Greek, "I have been posted here. I'm not in prison coincidentally. It didn't just happen. It isn't because political leaders weren't courageous enough to set me free when they knew I'd done nothing wrong. It wasn't happenstance. It wasn't circumstance. I am here under orders. I am stationed here by God. I am set for the defense of the Gospel!"

David says the same thing: "There is no surprise in this for a believer. God has separated the godly unto Himself, and nothing comes to the godly unless God has permitted or ordained it. God will take those circumstances and remake them."

One of my favorite writers is the late missionary-statesman E. Stanley Jones. In his book *The Way*, he tells the story of Dr. Lincoln Ferris.

Dr. Ferris' wife became infected when a medical doctor, who had just attended the childbirth of a diseased mother, failed to cleanse his instruments properly. It cost Dr. Ferris $30,000 (a fortune in that day!) and years of agony to restore his wife to a state of health. In the process, he nearly lost his faith.

He often asked God, "O God, why didn't You stop that doctor at the door?" Then, one day, as he was walking along the street, God spoke to him. Dr. Ferris later said it was almost an audible voice.

God said, "Can't you say what Jesus said: 'Father, into thy hands I commend my spirit'?" Before Dr. Ferris took another step, he uttered those words: "Father, into thy hands I commend my spirit." He said that from the depths of his heart his despair left, and he became a happy, victorious Christian again.

E. Stanley Jones, commenting on Dr. Ferris' experience, said: "From that moment, Dr. Ferris entered into life without a limp — *without a limp.*"

We must be able to say not only, "Lord, You can give me grace to endure this," but, "Lord, there is a reason why I am here. You are enlarging me in my distress. You have separated the godly unto Yourself." In other words, until there is a kind of rejoicing, there cannot be an ultimate joy and happiness. No wonder David follows those words with:

Be angry, and do not sin. Meditate within your heart on your bed, and be still.

Offer the sacrifices of righteousness, and put your trust in the Lord.

Psalm 4:5,6 *NKJV*

Paul uses this verse in the New Testament when he advises the Ephesians, "Be angry, and do not sin."

Here in Psalm 4 David is summoning the best of his spirituality, saying, "I will not allow my flesh to rebel against the will of God. I will protect what God is doing in my life. Spirit of David, commune with yourself on your bed! Take your strength from God instead of angrily arguing with God about your circumstances."

Then David says, "Offer the sacrifices of righteousness, and put your trust in the Lord" (verse 5). What sacrifice is God pleased with? Certainly it isn't the blood of bulls, goats, and heifers. As the Word of God cried out through the prophet Samuel to King Saul, "Obedience is better than sacrifice" (1 Samuel 15:22)."

Here in Psalm 4, David is saying, "The circumstances God has put me in are *right*. I don't want Him to change the circumstances. I want Him to change *me*. I am going to be enlarged. Room for me is going to be made through these circumstances. I am going to keep my spirit in check. I am not going to let the flesh bring me into a place of murmuring and complaining against what God is doing. I will offer the sacrifices of righteousness."

When David does that, the result is, "You have put gladness in my heart, more than in the season that their grain and wine increased" (Psalm 4:7). You don't have to be a scholar to understand that David is saying, "Here's the man who is really prospering! I have received more out of these God-ordained circumstances of suffering than anyone can receive from his wine and corn; his most prosperous moment."

This is the principle of brokenness in the believer's experience. *Brokenness is the costliest and most fragrant Christian virtue.* In a sentence, brokenness for a believer is learning to respond in humility and to accept the dealings and conviction of God. It comes from our willing response to God in our circumstances; not from a spirit of discontent, pouting, or anger.

Hebrews 12 teaches us that while some believers endure the chastening of God, being trained by it and discovering afterwards the peaceable fruit of righteousness, others become weary and discouraged, and even allow a root of bitterness to spring up in their lives, defiling many others.

I have often heard it said, "He only spoke five minutes, and I knew he was a man who had been broken." There is a mark of blessedness upon the life of a believer who has stood in his circumstances and been changed!

God is at work to enlarge you. The famous Scottish Bible scholar, Alexander Maclaren, wrote:

> Take care that you do not waste your sorrows; that you do not let the precious gifts of disappointments, pain, loss, loneliness, ill health, or similar afflictions that come into your daily life *mar you instead* of mend you [underlining our own].

I discover there are many wonderful Christians who are going to heaven, but they are marred because they have murmured, complained, and become bitter rather than seeing God in their circumstances. Rather than being enlarged by their circumstances, they have been diminished by something God intended for good to them who love Him. Romans 8:28 and 29 *(NKJV)* is true:

> **And we know that all things work together for good to those who love God, to those who are the called according to His purpose.**

> **For whom He foreknew, He also predestined to be conformed to the image of His Son, that He might be the first-born among many brethren.**

You may not like the sandpaper, and you may not like the chisel, but you must surely like the idea of being like Jesus. Keep your eye on the goal!

 PSALM 5

Give ear to my words, O Lord, consider my meditation.

Give heed to the voice of my cry, my King and my God, for to You I will pray.

My voice You shall hear in the morning, O Lord; in the morning I will direct it to You, and I will look up.

For You are not a God who takes pleasure in wickedness, nor shall evil dwell with You.

The boastful shall not stand in Your sight; you hate all workers of iniquity.

You shall destroy those who speak falsehood; the Lord abhors the bloodthirsty and deceitful man.

But as for me, I will come into Your house in the multitude of Your mercy; in fear of You I will worship toward Your holy temple.

Lead me, O Lord, in Your righteousness because of my enemies; make Your way straight before my face.

For there is no faithfulness in their mouth; their inward part is destruction; their throat is an open tomb; they flatter with their tongue.

Pronounce them guilty, O God! Let them fall by their own counsels; cast them out in the multitude of their transgressions, for they have rebelled against You.

But let all those rejoice who put their trust in You; let them ever shout for joy, because You defend them; let those also who love Your name be joyful in You.

For You, O Lord, will bless the righteous; with favor You will surround him as with a shield.

NKJV

Keep on Keeping On

I believe there is yet another imperative lesson from these Psalms about our time in between. Several verses from Psalm 5 establish this principle:

Give ear to my words, O Lord, consider my meditation.

Give heed to the voice of my cry, my King and my God, for to You I will pray.

My voice You shall hear in the morning, O Lord; in the morning I will direct it to You, and I will look up.

Psalm 5:1-3 *NKJV*

Verses 7, 8, and 11 *(NKJV)* go on to say:

But as for me, I will come into Your house in the multitude of Your mercy; in fear of You I will worship toward Your holy temple.

Lead me, O Lord, in Your righteousness because of my enemies; make Your way straight before my face...

But let all those rejoice who put their trust in You; let them ever shout for joy, because You defend them; let those also who love Your name be joyful in You.

What is the lesson in this fifth Psalm? Perhaps it seems more indirect than the others. David seems to be saying, "I learned in that moment when nothing seemed right, and all the promises of God seemed to be falling short of ever being achieved, to *keep on doing the things I knew to do.*

"I continued to meditate on the Word; I continued to cry unto God in intercession; I continued to pray, I continued to go into my house and turn my face toward the Temple; I continued to trust; and I continued to rejoice and praise God."

I feel sorry for Christians whose whole Christian life is based on *emotion.* They can praise and experience joy only when great joy is flowing among thousands of other praisers. They only hear from God when everything is going well. But when the cacophony of the world's voices sounds around them, they lose their victory and direction.

101

David seems to be saying, in paraphrase, "Don't ever doubt in the darkness what God said to you in the light." He is saying, "Hold on. Do the things you know to do."

Can you imagine David in those moments, surrounded by just a few counselors, while the thousands of Israel had gone over to Absalom's side? In the flesh, David might be pacing back and forth, saying, "What am I going to do? What kind of physical maneuver can I pull now? What kind of a political thing can I get hold of?"

But that isn't what David did. He continued to do the things he knew to do to maintain a relationship with God. He meditated on God's Word; he prayed and cried out to God; he trusted; and he continued to go to the house of God — to look toward the Temple.

There are certain things I consider most important to preserve in a church. I could not stay with a church which moved away from principles of tolerance toward one another. Nor could I be a part of a legalistic, man-made, traditional scheme which judges fellow believers on the basis of someone's personal convictions.

All believers will have problems and temptations. There will doubtlessly be sin. But stay in the fold; stay in fellowship. Have your problems *in* the church, not out of the church. The church is not a trophy case; it's a hospital!

The church is a place for people with problems. Keep coming to the temple — keep coming to the church — even when you're going through battles of doubt, and the enemy is pressing hard upon you. Keep these things uppermost: the Word in your heart, the church of God, and the fellowship of the saints.

Even if it takes all the courage you have to get up and go to church, don't stay away. Even if there are problems in your marriage, or if there has been a separation, don't stay away. Don't be afraid of how the "saints" will react to your problems. That is wrong!

The church is your home. It's where you belong. The Body of Christ should move all the more with its love, compassion, and concern when there are problems. David said, "I keep that lesson straight. When it gets dark, I just keep meditating, praising, praying, and crying unto God and trusting in Him."

I may truly call this book an anatomy of all parts of the soul, for no one can feel a movement of the Spirit which is not reflected in this mirror. All the sorrows, troubles, fears, doubts, hopes, pains, perplexities, stormy outbreaks by which the hearts of men are tossed have been depicted here to the very life.
—John Calvin
Commentary on the Psalms
1563

CHAPTER 9

The Joy of Repentance
(Psalms 3 Through 7)

*D*uring my days in Youth For Christ, I had a young friend named Bob. He was a committed and faithful part of my life and ministry. Eventually he became an Anglican minister.

When I knew him best, he was a delightful, but often crazy kind of person in some ways. His parents had given him a 1955 Ford, and when he learned to drive and would get into a tight situation which scared him, he would close his eyes, point the car straight ahead, and hope to get through. Believe me, I know this is true, because I've been with him when he did it!

This is exactly what many believers do. They get to a restricted situation, and they say, "Yes, there is a God, and I know I'm going to get through eventually — but I'm just going to close my eyes until I get through." They never see that the very circumstance itself is ordained of God. When David says, "God is making room for me out of this distress," he is admitting that the very circumstance, however difficult, enlarges a person.

"I've got to talk to my spirit and say to my soul, 'Now get with it; quit complaining,'" David says. "I commune with my spirit on the bed, and I tell my spirit, 'Accept what God's doing. Don't be angry about it, because God is at work in these circumstances.'" What a word! It's not only important to get down to the basics about God; it's important to get down to the basics of how God is using a specific set of circumstances in our time in between.

In his time in between, David had to learn a critical lesson, which he shares in Psalm 5. The superscription at the beginning of the Psalm is: "To the chief Musician upon Nehiloth." The word *nehiloth* could best be translated by the word "inheritance." (It may have also suggested a certain kind of a flute instrument with holes in it through which the breath would be blown to make a sound.)

David says in verse 1, "I have continued to meditate"; in verse 2, "I cried unto the Lord"; in verse 3, "I continue to pray"; in verse 7, "I'm going to the house of God in fear, and I'm worshipping toward the Temple"; in verse 8, "I'm continuing to get my guidance from God"; and in verse 11, "I have learned to trust, and I am praising God and rejoicing." Each of these establishes a unique and important pattern. In his time in between, David learned to keep doing what he knew to do.

We must never doubt in the dark what God reveals to us in the light. David is saying in essence, "One of the things I've learned during this awful time in between — the promise of God and its fulfillment between faith and victory — is simply to keep holding on and to do what God has always told me to do: to pray, to meditate upon the Word, to rejoice, to trust God, and to continue going into His house."

The lesson is to continue doing that which we know to be spiritually right, even when there are no answers, and heaven seems to be made of brass. Some people, however, seem to pray only when they get answers. Some only praise when the circumstances are right. They only enter into an experience of God when everything is somehow together. But David says, "I have learned in my time in between to *keep doing.*"

Some time ago, I studied Hebrews 10 in earnest. Verse 25 paraphrased was particularly revealing: "Not forsaking the assembling of ourselves together, *especially* so much the more as the day approaches." You could easily translate Hebrews 10:25, "Don't quit meeting with other believers when things get dark!"

When you are discouraged isn't the time to drop out of church. That's the time to come! When you're having trouble with sin, or when there's a problem in your marriage, that's not the time to say, "I don't want to face my friends." That's the time to *be there.* David said, "In that time in between I just continue to do the things I know to do spiritually."

As I was preparing this material, the Lord asked me, "Have you applied this?" And I was able to say, "Yes." I can think of many times in my life when there wasn't the warmth of emotion or the drive of success. There was simply the knowledge that a Christian prayed because prayer was right, and a Christian worshipped God not because of the circumstances, but because of who God is. A Christian went to the house of God not because he felt like it, but because he knew it was the hope he had, and he simply held on. David learned that lesson. May it quickly be the experience for all of us!

Psalm 6 gives us yet another issue to be faced. It is an especially important one. Psalm 6 is "The Psalm of Repentance" or "The Psalm of Chastisement."

In it, David voices such sentiments as, "O Lord, don't rebuke me in your anger; don't chasten me in displeasure. Have mercy...I'm weak...Heal me; my bones are vexed. My soul is vexed. Return, O Lord, deliver my soul...I am weary with groaning; all night I make my bed to swim and water my couch with tears. My eye is consumed with grief; it waxeth old...Depart from me, workers of iniquity...."

Seemingly, there is an answer in the middle of the Psalm: "The Lord hath heard the voice of my weeping" (verse 8); "The Lord hath heard my supplication; the Lord will receive my prayer" (verse 9); "Let all mine enemies be ashamed and sore vexed: let them return and be ashamed suddenly" (verse 10).

It is urgent for us to know that these times in between in our lives *must* always have a consciousness that God is working through that circumstance to bring us to a place of repentance.

PSALM 6

O Lord, do not rebuke me in Your anger, nor chasten me in Your hot displeasure.

Have mercy on me, O Lord, for I am weak; O Lord, heal me, for my bones are troubled.

My soul also is greatly troubled; but You, O Lord — how long?

Return, O Lord, deliver me! Oh, save me for Your mercies' sake!

For in death there is no remembrance of You; in the grave who will give You thanks?

I am weary with my groaning; all night I make my bed swim; I drench my couch with my tears.

My eye wastes away because of grief; it grows old because of all my enemies.

Depart from me, all you workers of iniquity; for the Lord has heard the voice of my weeping.

The Lord has heard my supplication; the Lord will receive my prayer.

Let all my enemies be ashamed and greatly troubled; let them turn back and be ashamed suddenly.

NKJV

Repentance is such a misunderstood concept; a negative concept for many. Many people would find it difficult to believe there is *joy* in repentance. That is what it is really meant to be and what David experienced in this Psalm. To many, repentance is the last thing to dig out of their spiritual duffel bag. *When nothing else works, bargain with God by repentance!*

A good marriage is based on constant, momentary communication. Unfortunately, that's not the way most of us act. When two people are married, one thing after another begins to affect them. They become hurt and misunderstood, and certain things are not done or are not followed through.

One partner, under these circumstances, puts the other in his or her "computer," and when that partner pushes the wrong emotional "button," his mate reads it all back: "Don't you remember in July 1967 you said so-and-so, and six months later you did such-and-such?" And the spouse stands there totally unbelieving that all this incredible memory could be there.

Other types of partners are offended when they go through the same experiences; however, they forget the details. They do not have that "computer" ability of memorizing. They simply become scarred. It's almost easier to deal with the clear memory. The other remembers only the hurt, the feeling of not being accepted, and the brutality of the situation. There is a permanent scar in their heart and psyche which they can't put their finger on.

Marriage, to be what God means it to be, demands a constant sense of communication and a sense of honesty to say, "Hey, I really didn't mean to say that," rather than walking away or rationalizing the hurt.

One writer, in a book which was a forerunner of a whole new concept of relational Christianity, wrote that for 17 years his marriage had centered around the garbage can!

He had been raised in a strong Southern family in which the man of the house did *nothing* about domestic matters. He brought home the paycheck and did the manly things, but he did nothing domestically. His wife, however, had been raised in a family where the man did nothing *except* take out the garbage. So for 17 years, they fought over the garbage pail.

Eventually, as all of you who know anything about marriage know, the issue got much bigger than the garbage pail. It became the whole issue of thoughtlessness, carelessness, and many other missing qualities. When this writer later became a born-again Christian before his wife did, he sought how he could testify to her concerning Christ. He thought about getting up at 5 o'clock in the morning and doing all kinds of spiritual things.

Finally he cried out in desperation, "O, Holy Spirit, how can I show her what it is to be a Christian?" The Holy Spirit said, *"Take out the garbage!"*

It's really usually that simple! In the time in between in our lives, God is at work trying to teach us something to bring us to repentance. Repentance in the believer's life is like communication ought to be in a marriage: instant and momentary! It isn't to wait until we have a big enough bag or enough accumulated sins to confess them, but instantly, "I've sinned in thought, or word, and action." Or perhaps, as the Word of God says, "I've omitted to do something I should have done. I've transgressed the Law, or I've thought something that wasn't of faith."

The Bible says that everything not of faith is sin. Sin is also falling short of the glory or purpose of God. It's important to be sensitive enough to immediately, naturally, and even joyfully empty our lives of these things.

I sustain my life by expelling from my lungs the old air or used up oxygen which has lost its value for life. I expel it back into the Earth so that through the process of working with green vegetative matter, that "death gas" or carbon dioxide may be turned back into oxygen. Then again I can breathe in that oxygen.

So many of us are continually breathing in oxygen, but we're not expelling carbon dioxide! It ought to be a normal, open, easy thing as I walk with the Lord but miss a step to say, "I missed that step, Lord." A Christian confesses his sin. The forgiveness is guaranteed in Christ. But you first must confess it, or, as the Greek word says, "You agree with God."

The prophet Amos asked, "Can two walk together, unless they are agreed?" (Amos 3:3). So in the time in between in my life, God is trying to make me aware of what repentance is all about. It's that momentary sense of, "Lord, I confess what was wrong, and I thank You for the blood of Jesus. I know what it cost You to make me righteous." Then go on!

Repentance is not only an awesome thing we do at great revivals, once every four years, or even once or twice in a lifetime; repentance is a momentary expression of expelling everything that is not according to Christ in our lives.

Perhaps the greatest definition of repentance is found in Second Corinthians 7. Paul loved this church at Corinth and had spent 18 months as its pastor. He was, in a sense, its founder. He called them "my children," and even said, "You are my joy and my crown." In essence, he was saying, "Everything I hope for is wrapped up in you."

Yet, as he moved away to minister in Ephesus, across a little bay, word came to him that the believers in Corinth were in dire trouble. Yes, they were spiritual. They prophesied, spoke in tongues, interpreted, and participated in other kinds of gifts of the Spirit. Yet they remained immature and even allowed a sin such as the Gentiles would not allow. A man had his father's wife in an adulterous relationship. It was probably not his mother, but even though it was a second marriage, it was incestuous in God's sight.

Paul wrote a burning letter in his first epistle to the Corinthians, asking, "How will you judge the angels? How will you judge me, since you can't even put an issue like this right in your own church?" His anger was real, and when the church got the letter, they fell apart! They not only put the thing right; they overcompensated. Finally the message came to Paul across the bay, saying, "This church has responded, but now they're overdoing it!"

Paul wrote a second letter and said in essence, "Now look, the man's already confessed. Restore him. Don't give Satan an opportunity to use this." Then he added:

> **For though I made you sorry with a letter, I do not repent, though I did repent; for I perceive that the same epistle made you sorry, though it were but for a season.**
>
> **Now I rejoice, not that you were made sorry, but that ye sorrowed to repentance; for ye were made sorry after a godly manner, that ye might receive damage by us in nothing.**
>
> **For godly sorrow worketh repentance to salvation not to be repented of; but the sorrow of the world worketh death.**
>
> **2 Corinthians 7:8-10**

If you want a genuine definition of "repentance," which is God's and not man's, look carefully at verse 11:

> **For behold this selfsame thing, that ye sorrowed after a godly sort, what carefulness it wrought in you, yea, what clearing of yourselves, yea, what indignation, yea, what fear, yea, what vehement desire, yea, what zeal, yea, what revenge! In all things ye have approved yourselves to be clear in this matter.**

There's repentance! Everyone can tell that. Clearing of yourselves, vengeance, and zeal to be clean before the Lord are characteristics of true repentance. And, Paul adds, "Because of the true repentance, you have the kind of sorrow which produces true deliverance."

114

I hardly need to state it, but all the repentance that goes on in a church is not godly sorrow. Often the repentance we see is the kind Paul calls "the sorrow of the world which works death." In other words, it's sorrow that we've been caught. It's a sorrow over consequences that things aren't working out.

God's judgment is upon us. We're suffering and receiving the results of what we have done, but we are not repenting over the offended righteousness of God. Repentance that is sincere ultimately has nothing to do with changing our circumstances; it's a change of our heart because of our identity with God.

We are saying, "Lord, I have offended You." That's where the vengeance, wrath, and zeal comes from. "Lord, You've been offended in this thing, and I sorrow in my heart that my actions, words, or thoughts have brought sorrow to You." There is the mark of true repentance.

Here is David in Psalm 6 running like a fugitive, his son having turned the hearts of Israel against him. But rather than pouting and stomping his feet like a disobedient child, David is saying, "Lord, there is a reason why this is happening. I will make my bed a flood of tears, and I will not cease to cry unto You day and night. I know You love me, and You are accomplishing a purpose in this for me." And only heaven could record the pleasure of God's heart!

Perhaps, as important as repentance is, we should see it from another viewpoint. In Hebrews 12:16 the writer says, "Lest there be any fornicator, or profane person, as Esau, who for one morsel of meat sold his birthright." One of the most misunderstood verses in the Bible is verse 17:

For ye know how that afterward, when he would have inherited the blessing, he was rejected: for he found no place of repentance, though he sought it carefully with tears.

I can almost hear it now: "How can God do that? Here is a man who was crying, yet God would not restore him."

115

We should probably ask, "Why was he crying?" We are clearly told that he didn't cry until he discovered that he had lost a temporal blessing. He didn't cry because he was no longer the patriarch of the family, or because he had given up spiritual blessings. He certainly didn't cry because God had been offended by his carnality and fleshliness.

He cried because in the process of losing the right to be the head of the family, he had thus lost cattle, money, and position. God says "I don't hear that kind of cry." That's the sorrow of the world which produces death. Esau sought by tears not to identify with God and truly repent, but to be sorry for the consequences of his action.

David learned in this time in between that God was doing something in his life. Hebrews 12:5,6 also speaks to this:

> **And ye have forgotten the exhortation which speaketh unto you as unto children, My son, despise not thou the chastening of the Lord, nor faint when thou art rebuked of him:**

> **For whom the Lord loveth he chasteneth, and scourgeth every son whom he receiveth.**

Every son God receives is being chastened. If you don't get the message positively, you get it negatively in the next two verses:

> **If ye endure chastening, God dealeth with you as with sons; for what son is he whom the father chasteneth not?**

> **But if ye be without chastisement, whereof all are partakers, then are ye bastards, and not sons.**

That's the negative. Without fail, every son receives chastisement. If you are not receiving chastisement, you are not a child of God. The writer continues in verses 9 and 10:

> **Furthermore, we have had fathers of our flesh which corrected us, and we gave them reverence: shall we not much rather be in subjection unto the Father of spirits, and live?**

> **For they verily for a few days chastened us after their own pleasure....**

When I was a boy, I believed somehow that my father disciplined me after his own pleasure. We all do at that point, I think.

...but he [God] for our profit, that we might be *partakers of his holiness.*

Now no chastening for the present seemeth to be joyous, but grievous: nevertheless afterward it yieldeth the peaceable fruit of righteousness unto them which are exercised thereby.

Hebrews 12:10,11

Perhaps we should ask an important question here: Does the chastening of the Lord profit all Christians? The answer is, of course, not! Hebrews 12 declares that the peaceable fruit of righteousness is only yielded in the lives of those who are *exercised* by the chastening.

Ask it again: Who profits? He who is *exercised*. There are believers who have gone around the same mountain time after time after time after time. God has brought discipline and chastening to their lives because He loves them and disciplines them. Yet they refuse to be exercised by what God is trying to teach, so God must say, in the words of one teacher, "Go around the mountain again!" (Take another turn around Mt. Sinai?)

Go around again and again and again, until finally there is some exercise by that chastisement. Then God can say, "You've learned. Now go on." How wonderful to hear that word!

We all must receive the admonition in Hebrews 12:12-14:

Wherefore lift up the hands which hang down, and the feeble knees;

And make straight paths for your feet, lest that which is lame be turned out of the way; but let it rather be healed.

Follow peace with all men, and holiness, without which no man shall see the Lord.

117

SALM 7

O Lord my God, in You I put my trust; save me from all those who persecute me; and deliver me.

Lest they tear me like a lion, rending me in pieces, while there is none to deliver.

O Lord my God, if I have done this: if there is iniquity in my hands,

If I have repaid evil to him who was at peace with me, or have plundered my enemy without cause,

Let the enemy pursue me and overtake me; yes, let him trample my life to the earth, and lay my honor in the dust.

Arise, O Lord, in Your anger; lift Yourself up because of the rage of my enemies, and awake for me to the judgment You have commanded!

So the congregation of the peoples shall surround You; for their sakes, therefore, return on high.

The Lord shall judge the peoples; judge me, O Lord, according to my righteousness, and according to my integrity within me.

Oh, let the wickedness of the wicked come to an end, but establish the just; for the righteous God tests the hearts and minds.

My defense is of God, who saves the upright in heart.

God is a just judge, and God is angry with the wicked every day.

If he does not turn back, he will sharpen His sword; He bends His bow and makes it ready.

He also prepares for Himself instruments of death; He makes His arrows into fiery shafts.

Behold, the wicked travails with iniquity, conceives trouble and brings forth falsehood.

He made a pit and dug it out, and has fallen into the ditch which he made.

His trouble shall return upon his own head, and his violent dealing shall come down on his own crown.

I will praise the Lord according to His righteousness, and will sing praise to the name of the Lord Most High.

NKJV

I want this to become obvious to you. David is sharing that during his time in between — a moment in which people said there was no help for him in God — he learned to be dependent on God and that God was his shield, not his emotions or experiences.

Second, David shares that he came to see that the very circumstances were ordained of God to enlarge him, and that enabled him to rejoice.

Third, David tells us, "I learned to keep on keeping on, to meditate on the Word, to pray, to rest in God, to turn my face toward the Temple, to keep doing what I knew to do spiritually, and not to cease during that moment."

In addition, David learned that God, in chastising him, was putting together a beautiful thing. David's bed became a place of tears, where he discovered true repentance and that the God who chastens is a God who loves.

You know the rest of the story. God eventually restored David, and his enemies were ultimately defeated. But when David returned to Jerusalem, he was a different man! He had learned in his time in between, and rather than becoming bitter and hard, God had completed a holiness in David's life. The latter days of his life were filled with great joy and rejoicing because of what the Lord had done.

Learning To Lean

Can we resolve an ultimate issue in Psalm 7? David basically says in this Psalm, "I have come to trust God. I am resting in the Lord." Perhaps the greatest ramification of this is found in verse 10, where David shares, "My defense is of God, and God saves the upright."

This ultimate lesson which David learned in his time in between is the lesson of *rest* — ceasing from his labor, his troubled, distorted, desperate, and despairing spiritual torment, and coming to rest and know peace through God.

I am told that the literal Hebrew for the portion of the verse which reads "My defense is of God" says, "My shield is upon God." Any man who did warfare then always had a shield-carrier or what was known as an armor-bearer. The reason for this was the multitude of different shields that were necessary for warfare.

Far distance fighting was done with a strong metal shield so a spear tossed a great distance could be warded off. Close-in fighting was done with another kind of shield. Thus, every warring man had an armor-bearer. David shares with us that a great final lesson he had learned was that his armor-bearer is God! His very defense was upon God. His shield was upon God.

An unfortunate choice of words was made in the sixteenth and seventeenth chapters of John in the *King James Version,* where the Holy Spirit, whom Jesus is going to send, is referred to as "a Comforter." Most of us think of "comforters" as the huge old quilts on grandmother's bed. Sleeping under those comforters made you get up feeling like you had been weight-lifting all night! That's *not* what the Holy Spirit is!

The literal word Jesus used in the Greek is *parakalaos* or *paraclete,* meaning "One who is called along beside you to help you." Jesus said, "It is expedient for you that I go away, for when I go away I shall send unto you another Comforter, another *paraclete.*" It is interesting that in the Greek, "another" means "One like unto the one you have," which was Jesus. So Jesus was saying, "Another One like Me will walk along beside you, carrying the shields. He will be your armor-bearer."

Perhaps this is an ultimate truth God must reveal to all believers in their time in between: that they don't have to defend themselves, excuse themselves, or rationalize their behavior. Can you imagine the temptation of David to try to explain how he, the king of that nation, was retreating like a fugitive before his own son, allowing a foul-mouthed prophet to curse and stone him, and not even allowing his nephew to take the man's life?

Try to imagine the place David reaches in this experience, during which he stands firm and says, "I have learned that my defense is upon God. My shield is on the Lord. He is enough."

There is a time in between in all of our lives. I have thought of several times like that. I once spent several hours with a dear woman whose husband served as secretary of the board of my church in Redwood City for 23 years. At one time he led its music program, and he was involved in many other church activities.

At Christmastime, while taking down lights, he fell from a ladder and experienced a head injury. He was rushed to the local hospital, where doctors confirmed brain damage and transferred him to another hospital a distance away to receive rehabilitation.

But during his stay in that facility, sitting in a wheelchair one day, he became confused and went out a door through the carelessness of those who were supposedly watching him, and somehow became caught on the fire escape area. Unable to get back in the door, he fell backwards down the flight of stairs and lay there 24 hours before he was discovered!

The doctors' final pronouncement to this dear saint was that there was no hope of change for her husband. As we talked for several hours, I was able to share with her that even David, in the 10th Psalm, cries out and says, "God, why do You hide from me? Where have You gone? What have I done that has caused You to hide from me?"

Whether you are young or old, I can assure you that there will be a time in between in your life, a time in between promise and fulfillment, a time in between revelation and its accomplishment, a time of waiting, gutting it out, learning and testing the very crucible in the nature of your spiritual experience.

You will either find dependency upon God or bitterness of spirit. David says to us, "In my time in between, which might have been filled with cursing and bitterness, saying, 'Where are You, God?' I instead grew in spiritual stature. I experienced holiness by means of repentance, and found that underneath me were the everlasting arms. I came to rest in God so that nothing the enemy throws at me now will cause me to turn back. I have gone through the worst, and I have discovered God in my life more deeply and meaningfully."

I once participated in a program run by a local police department. They trained and used some of us ministers as honorary police chaplains with all the medals to show for it! This particular police chief was one of the most aggressive in the United States.

As I sat in his office one day, talking to him about the program, I saw a plaque on the wall behind his desk. It read, *"No mariner distinguishes himself on a calm sea."* And so it is with us and with God! He can't make us giants without putting great loads on us and then helping us bear them. We must go through that time in between when God marvelously works out the will of the Holy Spirit in our lives.

[1] Alexander Maclaren as quoted by Lloyd John Ogilvie, General Editor, *The Communicators' Commentary, Psalms 1-72*. Word, 1986, p. 12.

The Laboratory of Life

SECTION 4

The Hope and Attitude Toward Mankind

(Psalm 8)

To regard nature as the symbol of God's glory is not at all strange or unnatural. It is, perhaps, the thing we are ultimately led to do when, thoroughly sophisticated, disillusioned, and disenchanted, we take ourselves seriously in hand and ask what is our business here. Then we stand confronted by the Ancient of Days.[1]

—F. J. E. Woodbridge

The Spirit of God is still witnessing through the Psalms, encouraging the godly to open themselves up for individual and collective transformation, requisite for Christian maturity and the worship of the living God.[2]

—Willem A Van Gemeren

PSALM 8

O Lord, our Lord, how excellent is Your name in all the earth, You who set Your glory above the heavens!

Out of the mouth of babes and infants You have ordained strength, because of Your enemies, that You may silence the enemy and the avenger.

When I consider Your heavens, the work of Your fingers, the moon and the stars, which You have ordained,

What is man that You are mindful of him, and the son of man that You visit him?

For You have made him a little lower than the angels, and You have crowned him with glory and honor.

You have made him to have dominion over the works of Your hands; you have put all things under his feet,

All sheep and oxen — even the beasts of the field,

The birds of the air, and the fish of the sea that pass through the paths of the seas.

O Lord, our Lord, how excellent is Your name in all the earth!

NKJV

CHAPTER 10

It Takes a Winepress
To Make Wine

(A Beginning Look at Psalm 8)

or some reason, the night overpowers us much more than the day, and that is often a positive recognition of the Creator's greatness. If you get away from the man-made lights of a city and walk under a darkened sky, perhaps halved only by a circle of pine trees, the vast darkness of the sky and the shadow of stars in their orbits become over-whelming.

It must have been that kind of moment for David as he walked alone under the stars on the very night in which he, as a young boy, had been used supernaturally by God to deliver the people of God from a great enemy.

What he wrote, however, was more than an epic creation poem. That recognition of God's work of creation is first and simplest for all of us: beauty, majesty, and grandeur!

David, in history, stands uniquely before the time of Christ on Earth, but after Adam. It was a period long before there was a Bible as such and certainly long before the cross of Redemption at Calvary. Yet here, this precocious and dedicated boy possesses within himself a divine ability to be in contact with God and to perceive spiritual truth.

David was as capable of revelation from God as Abraham was capable of a faith which would justify him before the Lord. Psalm 8 is thus more than meditation; this Psalm begins with a breakthrough recognition which is as strong as an emotional outburst.

"O Yahweh Adonai! O Jehovah, Ruler and Maker...how excellent is thy name in all the earth!" Psalm 8 contains no reference to sun or daytime revelations of creation; it mentions only the star-filled sky and the moon and the stars specifically as reflections of God. More than the timing is the reality. David experiences God. This is not maudlin worship of creation; it is inspired recognition of the Creator's greatness.

When David says in verse 3 that he considers, views, and understands, he is confessing what may be God's greatest gift to the human spirit. We can perceive: Having ears we can hear, and having eyes we can see.

The prophet Joel projected that when the Spirit of God comes upon mankind, young men shall see visions (Joel 2:28). When that prophecy is repeated in Acts 2, the simple Greek verb *horasis* is used, meaning they will have the ability to *see*. That must always be our prayer. It is a prayer which I have for you. Events and circumstances can often cloud our vision; even night itself may darken our spirit and depress our purpose. But God! He brings a moment of recognition which clears the doubt and gladdens the heart.

It seems to me that there are four "recognitions" in Psalm 8 which serve like tent pegs or ballasts for David's life. When he recognized these truths, they stabilized what might have been a very fragile and topsy-turvy life. David recognized the character and ability to know God, the power and excellence of His work, the declared and ultimate purpose of God in mankind, and the ultimate victory of God in everything He created. What phenomenal truths! What wonderful, life-stabilizing truths.

Interestingly, such a traumatic moment as David had experienced, with its life-threatening dimension (Goliath was no powder puff!) and its personal implications (the mistrust of family and the curiosity of others) could, in fact, become the very background for his moment of great recognition. I mention this so you, too, might have hope.

The superscription over Psalm 8 may be as important as the Psalm itself. Some commentators number these super-scriptions with the actual verses, since they may very well have been written by the original writers — something like the composer's expression marks on a new score of music. The superscription on Psalm 8 seems unusually important: "To the chief Musician upon Gittith, A Psalm of David."

This superscription has become a continuing controversy among students of biblical language and history. Is *Gittith* a musical instrument? One thing for sure, the word *Gittith* is connected with the province of Gath from which Goliath came. But Gath was also the area where David ran from Saul in that awful, seemingly endless period of his life, waiting for God's purpose to be fulfilled. David's victory over Goliath and his subsequent adulation by the women of Israel was the offense through which he was made an outlaw by Saul's jeal-ous anger.

So whether *Gittith* was a special musical instrument David became acquainted with while running from Saul (such as a Spanish guitar), the real instrument of Gath was not *musical* instrument. The experience associated with Gath was a moment when "the rubber hit the road," and the fantasies of childhood came face to face with the realities of life.

Gath may also literally mean "winepress." It is certainly in the family of words from which we get Gethsemane. Geth-semane actually refers to "the place of pressing olive oil." So Gath the place and *Gittith* the instrument may well be clues beyond psalmody or musical expression.

The fact remains that spiritual recognition is often as strong in change as an actual conversion. Such recognition or understanding is more often found in seasons of change and pressure.

The Greek New Testament often refers to a tribulation which is mandatory for all Christians. It is *thilipsis* in the Greek language, a word not at all implying actual imprison-ment or outright suffering. *Thilipsis* is probably best translated by the English word "pressure." *That* we all understand!

The force and crushing pressure of our Gaths may be dissimilar in detail, but they are always identical in potential. They are countries of change, places of released fragrance and spiritual growth, and arenas of recognition only, of course, if we recognize God in them, receiving His grace and following His syllabus!

When David says in Psalm 8:3 "When I *consider* [when I view, when I understand]," he is, in effect, giving the greatest prayer anyone can make for God's people — a prayer for them to have perception; having ears they can hear, and having eyes they can see.

We could paraphrase David's experience of recognition by saying, "O God, in this experience of my life I have learned how totally and perfectly righteous You are. I have learned how excellent and unsurpassed is your name, and how You have set your Word even above your name. I have learned and received something from your character. I have discovered something about You. I have come to recognize You even in places where You are not easily seen."

It's a mind-boggling experience when Sunday School knowledge and "churchianity" falls off like a shackle, and there suddenly comes a personal recognition! The individual perceives God. He experiences His character, His righteousness, trustworthiness, faithfulness, love, and mercy. It's recognition!

People seldom understand when someone in the church really has this kind of experience with God. You will even hear others say, "I've known that all along." And you can tell by the way they say it that they may know the *fact*, but they don't know the *experience*. They don't understand the experience, because it cannot come from head knowledge.

David knew and was trained from a boy, "Yahweh is holy." God's name could not even be pronounced! But now Yahweh was personal. The language is almost romantic and intimate. Through his experience, God had become imperatively recognizable to David: "O Yahweh Adonai."

Yahweh is the One who causes to be — the Ruler! How excellent is thy name! Thank God from time to time when someone gets "turned on." It would be wonderful if every believer in a church would get turned on at least once! Of course, they don't. But thank God when there's the cry "O Yahweh Adonai!" from a person who has been in the church 20 years — or even two weeks. They cry out, "O Yahweh Adonai! O Jesus, Lord! I see You. I've heard about You. I went to Sunday School and they talked about You, but now I *know* You! It's personal."

Even the Greek New Testament used different words for "knowledge" — one meaning "facts" and another meaning experiential knowledge. Ultimately, there had to be a new word, so the word *epignosis* was made or used. It actually means "to move toward knowing," or, in other words, intimacy of progressive personal knowledge. The experience is continual and not just intellectual, as in marriage.

In this Psalm, David also recognized God's work. God's character is inseparably bound to what He does. First, David saw the heavens, the skies, the stars, and the moon. And ultimately he realized man as God's unique workmanship. A part of God's new work in David's life was for him to recognize *God in man*. David experienced a recognition of the greatness of God revealed in His plan and mercy toward man.

What "Gath" experience will it take for many of us to release our theological comfort zone for a balanced biblical view of human life? Like the blind man of Bethsaida, the first touch from Jesus gave him the ability "to see men as trees, walking." Only the second touch allowed him to see men as men.

Oh, how we need to see true purpose in human life — God in shoes! Then we will no longer point the finger at men and women in their sin and immorality. Instead, we will find an endless fountain of tears to see the craftsmanship of God, the invention of the spirit, distorted, unrealized, and ultimately unfulfilled.

David's perception went deeper still in Psalm 8. He also saw man's destiny, man's fulfillment, and man's hope. Three times in the original Hebrew and twice in the English, the word "ordained" is used. Today that word is used in a very select sense. We ordain ministers or elders, but, in reality, the word "ordain" means simply "to put or to place."

David is saying, in effect, "I see now that God has placed this creation or ordained it. He has set it and established it. And perhaps, greatest of all for David — as it would be for most of us — was to say, "He has also ordained man. He has set man with the ultimate purpose of subduing the Earth and having all things under his feet." Man's hope! Humanity's destiny!

David also saw in Psalm 8 that the ultimate issue was God's glory. He ends the Psalm by crying again, as he began, "Yahweh Adonai, how excellent is thy name in all the earth!"

These four recognitions are like tent pegs to help keep the circus tent of our lives on the ground. David saw and recognized the character and work of God, the ultimate purpose of man, and the ultimate glory of God. When he realized these truths, his otherwise fragile and topsy-turvy life became stabilized.

I believe the list of faith heroes in Hebrews 11 is an example of this same recognition. You are familiar with the contents of Hebrews 11: "By faith Abel...by faith Enoch...by faith Noah...by faith Abraham...by faith Sarah...by faith Isaac...by faith Jacob...by faith Moses...by faith Rahab," and so forth.

In biblical truth, faith and hope are Siamese twins; you cannot have one without the other. Our preaching often emphasizes faith without teaching about *hope*. Why did Abraham leave his home country to go into another? Because by the eyes of faith he was given hope concerning a city that had foundations being built by God.

His faith was not a nebulous concept of religious pie-in-the-sky. His faith was based on the solid hope of what God had shown him and what would be the hope concerning man, his purpose, and his destiny. That's an absolute prerequisite to true faith that moves us into the glory and the purpose that God has for us.

David had known and served God. He had sung about God. But suddenly he comprehended God. God was in the language of his own personal experience. I often listen to Christians talk about death. As a pastor, I must constantly watch Christians walk through the valley of the shadow of death with loved ones. They walk as far as they can down the road, and then, surrendering the hand of their loved one into the hand of One uniquely pierced by a nail, they must turn and walk away.

The difference between a Christian talking about death and a Christian who has walked the valley of the shadow of death and found the Lord faithful is the difference between talking to a nursery school student versus a graduate student in trigonometry. David, in this Psalm, apprehends God personally! "O Lord, your character, your works, your purpose for me, your ultimate glory...."

This comprehension changes David! He is given the hope upon which his faith will rest, and with these two (faith and hope), David becomes a vessel capable of being used. His childhood has passed; his religiosity is over; and he is now into a true spiritual experience. No wonder David says, at the beginning of this Psalm, "This is a Psalm about a winepress. This is a Psalm whereby you understand that the grapes are crushed, so that the fragrant aroma of the wine may be shared."

Let's face it: *A believer cannot give what he does not have!* Wine can't come from a life which has refused the press. All the glory God has to reveal to you is to be pressed from the experience of the now — from the Gath of your life and your experience. God takes that Gath experience and produces a song of life which becomes an inheritance for the world.

God so desperately wants to come forth from a textbook relationship with you! He so desperately wants to come forth even from the Bible and to be apprehended by faith in a person's experience. He wants to be *your* God. Tens of thousands of people have cried, "O Yahweh Adonai!"

He's waiting to hear you cry, "O Lord, *my* Lord; how excellent is thy name in all the earth! When I consider your character, your works, and your purpose for *me*, and your ultimate glory, I am changed from glory unto glory in the image You wish me to be."

We stress the Humanity of Christ too exclusively at Christmas, and the Deity too exclusively after the resurrection... The ancient interpretation of Psalm 8, however arrived at, is a cheering corrective.[3]

—C. S. Lewis

CHAPTER 11

A Rumor in the Pig Pen

*A*s long as I can remember, thinking back to the earliest recollections of childhood fantasy, there has been a strong, recurrent prevailing power or ability which belonged only to fantasy; never to real life.

It was a prevailing ability which was a part of my unconscious dream world. Whatever circumstance imposed itself upon my dreams — whether the necessity of flight, or the simple joy of experiencing something — I was given the ability to bound into the air as though spring-powered on my feet. I could leap over buildings in a single bound!

That fantasy was so real to me. It was an emotion of lightness, power, and joy. I would awaken and feel as if I could actually go out and experiment with doing it. I was sure I could do what my dreams had told me and just spring to my victory and spring away from my captors!

Most readers will smile at this. It doesn't take much psychoanalysis to understand its meaning! It is equally not surprising to know that the frequency of that particular vision, that wish-fulfilling fantasy, has been in inverse proportion to my age. The younger and earlier I was in life experience, the more frequently that dream occurred; and the older I became in years, the less was its frequency. Advancing age has almost completely annihilated it. In fact, I don't even remember the last time I sprang over a building with one flying leap!

Psalm 8 is an incredibly sensitive and important Psalm which somewhat helps interpret my fantasy and the hopes of others. We have already seen that Psalm 8 is the second great Messianic Psalm, explaining when the Son of man, who has been rejected, will have all things put under His feet.

In that sense, Psalm 8 is the ultimate fulfillment of the victory of the Messiah Christ. It is a forerunner passage to Philippians 2, which says, "One day every knee shall bow and every tongue shall confess Him Lord" (verse 10). Indeed, the Spirit of God expressly teaches us in Hebrews 2 that Psalm 8 applies to Jesus Christ, the Messiah, by quoting it in that context. It is the ultimate plan and purpose of the Father that we do not yet see all things under His feet. All things will ultimately rest in Christ's control. We dare not limit ourselves, however, to that singular understanding, as exalting to the Lord as it is.

David is also in Psalm 8. He is recalling a literal night following a great deliverance in his life; perhaps the very night after he had been used of God to conquer the giant Goliath. That may explain the reason for the use of the word *Gittith* at the beginning of the Psalm. *Gittith* is associated with Gath, the province from which Goliath came. He was the giant of Gath. David is in this Psalm, perhaps walking under the starry canopy of heaven, being especially mindful of the greatness of Jehovah God. He has also seen that Jehovah God chooses to use *man* as an instrument of His purpose. That must have been a life-changing moment for David.

But there is another player here. Israel is also in this Psalm — that bobbing, seemingly unsinkable cork which is tossed about by all the raging waters of the human tide; that land and people who have been crushed, broken, ground, and dispersed, but who never cease to hope and believe that ultimately they have a place in the divine dominion and direction of the world.

Mankind, in general, is also in this Psalm. You and I are in Psalm 8! Someone once said, "Hope springs eternal in the human breast." It does! I know that mankind is sinful, sullen, and prideful. I know that man can sink to unbelievable lows of inhumanity and violence. But, like the prodigal son who is about to reach for and fill his body with the carob pods which the hogs were eating, mankind keeps hearing an inveterate rumor — a rumor that simply won't go away — a rumor that is firmly established — even in the hog pen.

That rumor says that mankind is different, belongs to a different family, and cannot be satisfied with hog swill. Like my recurring fantasy, the springiness, the power to rise up, is known deep in the breast of mankind. He is not *of* the Earth. *There is a remainder of heavenly atmosphere in man's lungs!*

Many have spent years breathing the smog of this world and with it even the fragrance of the hog pen, yet there is an atmosphere left over in man's lungs. It's the remembrance and nostalgia of the fragrance of heaven that says man belongs to another world and is part of another kingdom. As a result, man has another destiny. Perhaps the statement in Genesis 1 is the best summary: "In the beginning *God* created man." In a sense, Psalm 8 is a devotional commentary on Genesis 1, so let's review some of those verses:

> **And God made the beast of the earth according to its kind, cattle [domestic animals] according to its kind, and everything that creeps on the earth according to its kind. And God saw that it was good.**

> **Then God said, "Let Us [plural tense Father, Son, and Holy Spirit]** *make man in Our image, according to Our likeness;* **let them have dominion over the fish of the sea, over the birds of the air, and over the cattle [tame beasts], over all the earth, and over every creeping thing that creeps on the earth."**

> **So God created man in His own image; in the image of God He created him; male and female He created them.**

> **Then God blessed them, and God said to them, "Be fruitful and multiply; fill the earth and subdue it; have dominion over the fish of the sea, over the birds of the air, and over every living thing that moves on the earth."**

> **And God said, "See, I have given you every herb that yields seed which is on the face of all the earth, and every tree whose fruit yields seed; to you it shall be for food.**

Also, to every beast of the earth, to every bird of the air, and to everything that creeps on the earth, in which there is life, I have given every green herb for food"; and it was so.

Then God saw everything that He had made, and indeed it was very good [very suitable, very pleasant and He approved it completely]. So the evening and the morning were the sixth day.

Genesis 1:25-31 *NKJV*

We have earlier suggested that Psalms 3 through 7 are like a bridge, the time in between prophecy and fulfillment, the promise and the realization, the faith and the eventual victory. We have looked at it in four perspectives: First, a time in between for *David*, written in that awful moment of his flight before Absalom; second, for *Israel*, applying to the time leading up to Israel's acknowledgment of the Messiah; third, *the Messiah* Himself, first rejected and then eventually purposed to rule with all the nations of the world under His feet.

Fourth, remember that bridge also applies to the time in between for *us!* And again that's why Psalm 8 is so strategic. It is hope and more than that, *the* hope. It is the very belief, the gut-level knowledge that there is a fulfillment coming — an eventual fulfillment of the promises of God for all mankind, including ourselves.

Many people don't really "have their act together." If you are one of these people, you recognize your sinfulness. Perhaps you are often desperate and disappointed in yourself and in life. Some human beings even contemplate suicide. Things often seem hopeless in the time in between. Yet there remains that persistent rumor in men's hearts that simply won't go away, even for non-believers — those without a revelation of Jesus Christ — those who really do not know the Word of God.

There is still something eternally buried down in the human spirit which declares man is meant for greatness; he was created in the image of God; and there is great purpose in human life. This is like a divine spark within man which cannot be submerged or drowned in all the cacophony of sounds in the world. Neither can it be drowned by the waves of temptation that sweep over the human soul.

Unfortunately, contemporary theology is so wrapped up with the fall of man in Genesis 3 that it has completely forgotten the creation and ultimate purpose of man in Genesis 1! Words like "original sin" and "total depravity" have robbed many of us of a correct sense of the original purpose and divine human intention which God means for mankind.[4]

The psalmist here in Psalm 8 exclaims a familiar question for all of us: "What is man, that thou art mindful of him? And the son of man, earth-born man, that You should care for him?" Or, as the *King James Version* says, "That thou visitest him?" The end of the question is an affirmative answer. It is not a question without an answer. Actually, the question is rhetorical.

The psalmist is saying in wonderment, "Why do You care? Why do You visit? Why are You mindful?" But the conclusion is that God *is* mindful of man. God *has* visited man and has a purpose for him. This is a conclusion that is entirely different from what many people reach. There are endless dialogues on human disparity, often from the pulpit or from our teachers, to tell us we have become distorted.

There is a perverted sense that has come from some distorted theology which in essence has altered this truth of God's creation. The Bible declares that mankind is created in the image of God. What does God's creation of man mean?

In the Old Testament, the prophet Zechariah said:

The burden of the word of the Lord for Israel, saith the Lord, which stretcheth forth the heavens, and layeth the foundation of the earth, *and formeth the spirit of man within him.*

Zechariah 12:1

Ecclesiastes 12:7, speaking of death, says:

Then shall the dust return to the earth as it was: *and the spirit shall return unto God who gave it.*

---

[4] I am reminded of a scene from Franco Zeffirelli's film "Brother Sun, Sister Moon" (Euro-International Films, 1972), in which Alec Guiness as Innocent III gives his papal blessing to Saint Francis of Assisi with the words, "In our obsession with original sin, we too often forget original innocence."

And Genesis 2:7 says:

And the Lord God formed man of the dust of the ground, and breathed into his nostrils the breath of life; and *man became a living soul.*

There are so many technologically sophisticated facts which we know about evolution and biological reproduction. But beyond such technical knowledge there is the simple biblical belief that at some divine point in the life of an embryo, God supernaturally breathes into that child the breath of God Himself; that each child becomes *a living soul*, not simply a biological or animated life which joins other forms of animal life.

With the borrowed breath of God, the borrowed nature of God, that embryo becomes a form of God, created in and stamped with the image of the divine God Himself. God breathes into the nostrils the breath of life!

However fallen, however distorted, however sinful man is, there is in every man that borrowed nature of God which is His divine spirit, the breathed nature of God. And however perverted it becomes, that nature is there. When death comes, that spirit returns to God from whom it was borrowed to begin with. Seeing that, understanding that, is the most imperative understanding for believers who want to deal honestly with people.

To some Christians, people don't seem to *exist* until they become born again. Often that attitude toward the lost is as though they are non-people who can only become valuable when they are born again through the Spirit of God. *That is not true!* There is in every man, woman, boy, and girl, however perverted and sinful, however distorted and destitute, that borrowed nature of God which is the very spark of divine life. This must be the truth that reached the great hymn writer, Fanny J. Crosby, when she wrote the following words:

Down in the human heart, crushed by the tempter,
Feelings lie buried that grace can restore;
Touched by a loving heart, wakened by kindness,
Chords that are broken will vibrate once more.
Rescue the perishing, care for the dying;
Jesus is merciful, Jesus will save.[5]

Although blind, this woman lived in such daily communion with God by the Holy Spirit that she could "see" more clearly than many sighted persons. She understood this divine revelation: that in every human life — in every person we see — there lie buried and crushed by temptation and the enemy, feelings that divine grace can quicken. Divine grace can restore life and music again to human beings!

I have discovered in my own life what this theological prejudice is like. I have seen its obnoxious character in me as I watched in airplanes and terminals people who, up to this point, my response has been so negative toward. Their language, their deeds, their habits, or what they were involved in have always repulsed me.

However, since the Holy Spirit has begun to restore this understanding, it is easy for me to look across the room at a person who epitomizes all that is against my nature, yet begin to pray, "Lord, down in that human heart, crushed by the tempter, buried by sin, buried by habit, there is a divine spark of God's life. Holy Spirit of God, quicken that life. Bring that person some word of kindness, some deed, some act of love that will quicken those dying chords, that the divine spark may become inflamed again, and that the image of God may be seen."

Christians must be careful about being prejudiced toward anyone created in the image of God. The human spirit, that borrowed nature of God, lies there waiting to be quickened, although dead in trespasses and sins. It is but a quickening breath for that person to be what God intended him to be. No wonder Job exclaimed, "But there is a spirit in man: and the inspiration of the Almighty giveth them understanding" (Job 32:8).

It is helpful at this point to declare something: Whatever man's decisions, however far he runs, there is no ultimate way to escape this. There is clearly a preference and impact of sin. The power of evil is undeniably strong. *But* I choose to also know the value of a human soul. However dirty, however stepped upon, however mud-covered a diamond is, it will always remain a diamond. When it is taken out of the wrong context and carefully cleansed, it will radiate with all the purity and value that it has.

So there is a spirit within man — there is a borrowed nature of God in you. Crush it, break it, run from it, cover it, and hide it — but it is still there. And that nature of God always makes the miracle of transformation an instant possibility.

Let's start out right. The rumor mankind has heard is true! We were not born to the gutter, but to glory. There is a divine genetic. Satan may usurp power over man, but he did not create man. Satan may control man, but he cannot breathe life into him. That only comes from God.

The restlessness in the spirit of man is homesickness for God, and there will never be peace for man until he has rested his heart in the harbor of the Lord.

I am simply a poor man who seeks his God, sobbing and calling Him along all roads.[6]

— Contemporary French
poet Leon Bloy

CHAPTER 12

Recognition and Revelation

H. G. Wells told an amusing story entitled "The Soul of a Bishop." In this work of fiction, he listens to a conversation between a bishop and an angel.

The angel is telling the bishop that all religions are trying to express a truth which they don't clearly know. The angel goes on to tell him that there is a mystical "something" which eludes the mind like water escapes the hand.

At this, the bishop, who is hoping for some exclusive revelation of truth from God, cries out and says, "But you can tell me the truth!"

The angel simply smiles, cupping his hands over the bishop's bald spot, and strokes it affectionately. Then, holding the bishop's cranium in his strong hands, the angel says, "Truth? Yes, I could tell you the truth, but could you hold it in this little box of brains? You haven't anything to hold it inside with."

That story is both true and false, for man *is* capable of discovering reality. Man has, as it were, built into him a radio receiver. He has a God-built antenna which is pointed toward the stars. But, unfortunately, man cannot figure out the truth for himself. He has the receiver, but not the amplifier. He cannot *originate* the truth; he can only *receive* it as it is revealed.

That's where man is deceived. When mankind tries to figure it out for himself, he muddles the interpretation. But when he tunes in and listens, he delights. In other words, man can receive only when he has revelation. He is capable of recognizing and acknowledging truth. He has a "receiver" for truth, but there must first be divine revelation.

Yes, there is a God-image inside every man and woman — more crushed in some; more denied in others; covered with silt, sin, and smog in still others. But that God-nature allows man to recognize the truth of God's revelation.

The first chapter of Romans is perhaps the most important scriptural discussion concerning sin's universal curse. It is, in a sense, a general survey of the religious history of the human race from the very beginning. It declares that man at first, in his earliest days, was monotheistic.

That is certainly not what is taught in contemporary education! There we are taught that primitive man's religion began with some sort of fetishism, then became polytheistic, and only gradually evolved to a point of monotheism. God says no! Man began with a total monotheistic relationship with God — one God! Only when he rejected truth did mankind devolve (my own word). He went down the scale from monotheism to polytheism and eventually to fetishism.

Let us look at Romans 1:17-21 *(NKJV)*:

For in it the righteousness of God is revealed from faith to faith; as it is written, "The just shall live by faith."

For the wrath of God is revealed from heaven against all ungodliness and unrighteousness of men, who suppress the truth in unrighteousness,

because what may be known of God is manifest in them, for God has shown it to them.

For since the creation of the world [and every believer needs to know this as well as he knows anything in the Bible] His invisible attributes are clearly seen, being understood by the things that are made, even His eternal power and Godhead, so that they are without excuse,

because, although they knew God, they did not glorify Him as God, nor were thankful, but became futile in their thoughts, and their foolish hearts were darkened.

Did you ever notice the five steps by which God abandons mankind in Romans 1? What happened? Romans 1:28 says because man would not keep the truth he knew, and because he did not want to remember God, God gave him a reprobate mind so he would ultimately have a blotted-out concept of what he once knew.

Pay particular attention to the next few statements of this important argument. It is one of the most important things we can deal with. This is God's statement of history. We needn't argue for God. How presumptuous! God says here through the apostle Paul that man went from monotheism to fetishism, from a perfect knowledge of God to a total reprobate mind in which he did not remember God.

There is also an obvious microcosmic sense applying to the Roman Empire in the first chapter of Romans. At the time the Book of Romans was written, Roman civilization was in a final stage in its development. Arnold Toynbee once counted 21 separate civilizations in the 6000-8000 recorded years of man's history. He writes that every one of the 21 has followed the same pattern so closely, you could lay them over each other like transparencies. He writes:

> Thus the increasing command over the environment which an ironic or malicious or retributive Providence is apt to bestow upon a society in disintegration only serves, in the end, to put a greater driving power into the suicidally demented society's chosen work of self-destruction; and the story turns out to be a simple illustration of the theme that "the wages of sin is death."[7]

But this book is not about philosophy or history. In a true microscopic sense, Romans 1 is about *us*. It is about individuals — choice, truth, revelation. And what happens? Here is the original dichotomy which separates the world: a progression of faith to faith to righteousness (verse 17); and/or wrath and rebellion to sin and ultimate destruction. There are really two choices given in Romans 1. Some people activate faith in what they know and take the next steps God reveals. Faith reveals each step, and these persons move toward righteousness. Others, by rebellion, move from sin to sin to sin to wrath. Clearly, the two key words of this passage are "revealed" and "progressive."

Everything God has done, He has revealed: "The righteousness of God is revealed" (verse 17), and "the wrath of God is revealed" (verse 18). No closet, no hidden thing — it is God's proclamation.

How long has this revelation been known? Since the creation! To whom is it revealed? To all who were made, to those who are created, to the entire creation! What do they know? His eternal Godhead and His power. Thus, they are without excuse in not receiving.

Theologians divide revelation into two categories: *general* revelation and *special* revelation. Psalm 19 is a clear biblical text concerning general revelation. It confirms what Paul teaches in Romans 1: From the creation of the world, God *has* revealed His person and His power to all the creation.

The heavens declare the glory of God; and the firmament shows His handiwork.

Day unto day utters speech, and night unto night reveals knowledge.

There is no speech nor language where their voice is not heard.

Their line has gone out through all the earth, and their words to the end of the world. In them He has set a tabernacle for the sun.

Psalm 19:1-4 *NKJV*

The Hebrew word for "declare" is *caphar* (saw-far'). It means to recount or recall, to make a tally of something, or to inscribe as by a writer. The heavens inscribe something like a writing. The heavens recount something and make a daily tally of something.

What is it? "The firmament shows His handiwork." Here the Hebrew uses the word *nagad* (naw-gad'), which means to stand out boldly or to make something manifest. We might say "to certify" or "to guarantee." The firmament, which is the heavens, guarantees, certifies, and makes known His handiwork.

The phrase "Day unto day utters speech" in the Hebrew is *naba* (naw-bah'). It means "to gush forth, to pour out, to utter with abandon." Day unto day there is a gushing out of speech!

The fourth word we might need to know comes from Psalm 19:2: "Night unto night reveals knowledge." In the *King James Version,* the word "sheweth" is used. It is the Hebrew *chavah* (khaw-vah'). It means to make something clearly evident so anyone may understand it. Again:

> **There is no speech nor language where their voice is not heard.**
>
> **Their line** [that is the Hebrew word *qav* (kav), meaning "their lawyer's argument, their proof, their analysis of truth] **is gone out through all the earth, and their words to the end of the world. In them He has set a tabernacle for the sun** [the light].
>
> **Psalm 19:3,4 *NKJV***

Any person who begins to witness concerning his faith in Jesus Christ will ultimately use such verses as, "For all have sinned and fall short of the glory of God" (Romans 3:23); "There is none righteous, no, not one" (Romans 3:10); and "For the wages of sin is death, but the gift of God is eternal life in Christ Jesus our Lord" (Romans 6:23 *NKJV*).

It is almost guaranteed that as the Holy Spirit begins to focus in on that unsaved person, he or she will inevitably try to change the subject! The method most often used is to bring up the subject of the lost in Africa. "What about people who have never heard of Jesus Christ?" they ask. "Are you telling me this is the only way to God? What about all those people who have never heard?"

How many tens of thousands of times has that argument been brought up? It is like the woman at the well who, when Jesus pointed out her sin, tried to steer Him into a discussion on religion. This old trick is always used to change the subject. Psalm 19 in simple eloquence declares that no speech or language, no isolated position in the world, is exempted from a daily and nightly abundant revelation of God's glory and purpose. *Wherever the creation of God exists, there is abundant revelation of who God is!*

Immediately there are those who say, "But that's not enough!" You're right! No man is born again by seeing the general revelation of God. Mankind's sinfulness had to be accounted for. That's why the Son of God came and died ignominiously on the cross of Calvary. General revelation is not enough, but it is a first step. Again read what God says in Romans 1:17: "...righteousness...is revealed from faith to faith." When mankind takes the first step, it is the promise of God to lead from that step to the next one.

There is a marvelously documented missions account of Sammy Morris, a boy in the farthest jungles of the Congo a century ago. No white man had ever visited his village — no Bible, no missionary, and no "revelation," as we say. By his own account, Sammy Morris as a little boy walked out under the great general preacher of the heavens.

He said, in effect, "This was not made by the sticks which we worship. This was not made by the god of our hands." He proclaimed on the nature of this revelation that there was a great God. That God led that simple child step by step until several months later he walked into a missionary compound more than 130 miles away.

The first thing he said to the missionaries, through a servant piecing together bits of dialect, was, "I have come that you may tell me of the Holy Spirit." The missionaries asked, "How do you know about the Holy Spirit?" The little boy began telling them things which caused them to realize he knew more than they could have imagined. They ultimately sent him to America for deepening education and knowledge.

Several years ago when visiting the Harvard Library, I had the privilege of seeing one of three copies in existence of a documented testimony of a Siamese woman who had lived in the most dense darkness one could imagine. In a sense, she was living in a culture that was at the bottom of the latter portion described in Romans 1: a reprobate mind.

Still, there was in her that image of God which could recognize truth. In essence, she cried out, "God is God. There is a God who is not one of these idols. He is not what we put on the fronts of our homes. There is an eternal God who made us." Upon this declaration, on a step-by-step basis of that faith, God led her until one night Jesus Christ personally appeared to her. This is what theologians call "a Christophany." It is similar to what happened to the apostle Paul himself.

Several years ago, a woman from a Moslem background spoke in the pulpit of the church I pastor. She had an almost identical story: no missionary, no Bible, and no one spoke truth to her in any way, yet she had a heart which cried out, "There must be a God." She, too, moved out on the basis of the general revelation. God led her step by step, faith to faith, until righteousness, and Jesus Christ revealed Himself to her.

The Word of God indicates that no man will ever respond to general revelation but that God will reveal the next step to him if his heart has been sincere in acknowledging the truth. Abraham is a great case in point.

Abraham, tradition says, was the son of a man who made idols. Certainly Joshua 24 says that he "served other gods." Perhaps with his own hands he helped his father make these idols. One day in the despair of his human heart, the heart of a man made in the image of God with a ability to certify, realize, and recognize truth, he went in and began to knock down these hand-made idols.

Perhaps he cried, "If any of you be gods, strike me dead!" Ultimately, Abram, as he was then called, must have cried, "God, reveal Yourself to me." The story is clearly documented in Genesis, Isaiah, Romans, and Hebrews. This is certainly the story of a man living in total darkness who responded to general revelation and was led by God to specific revelation. "For what does the Scripture say?" Paul asks in Romans 4:3. "Abraham believed God, and it was accounted to him for righteousness."

Recently a young man who knew nothing about spiritual things came into one of our services. No one had invited him. He had spent most of his adult life in prison, experiencing drugs and every form of debauchery one could imagine.

One night in prison, not because of any spiritual revelation, but simply through a deep spiritual hunger, he said, "I had a vision in which I experienced the vastness of God, and a hunger was created in my life. I came to church because of that hunger, and it was as though the whole sermon was directed right to me!" Again, when a person responds by faith to that which he *does* know, he will be led from faith to faith to faith to righteousness.

The psalmist cried out this tremendous, incredibly important word: "The heavens, the moon, the sun, the stars which You have made with Your own hands, declare to me, and I recognize them. They lead me to cry, 'O Yahweh Adonai, O Lord, Thou art Master; Thou art Lord of the universe!'"

All men don't do that. The spirit within man does not lead all men to acknowledge truth. In fact, many men get caught up in this ability to have rational thought. It's a God-given ability, but we begin to make it a god itself. The agnostic Robert Ingersoll, standing at the grave of his brother, cried out, "Life is a narrow vale between the cold, barren peaks of two eternities. We strive to look beyond their heights; we cry aloud, and the only answer is the echo of our wailing cry."

Jean Paul Richter wrote, "I have traversed the world. I have risen to the suns. I have passed athwart the great waste places of the sky. There is no God! I have gazed into the gulf beyond and cried: 'Where art thou?' And no answer came." His last line is, "We are orphans, you and I; every soul in this vast corpse trench of the universe is utterly alone."[8]

Mark Twain once sneered, "Special providence! The phrase nauseates me! God doesn't know that we are here, and he would not care if he did!"[9] Many members of the human race, created in the image of God, see something different because of their inordinate affection for their own mind.

I cannot say that this image of God-ability, hidden in the spirit of man, inevitably leads man to recognize God. I only know *it is capable* of recognizing God. God has revealed Himself, but man must act upon that revelation. Man must *do* something!

There is doubtless a perverted evangelicalism, a hyper-fundamentalism, which denies by its very nature things which God asserts; namely, that man is capable of responding. The Fall did not change the purpose or breath of God in the spirit of man. Others have moved beyond the recognition that revelation is consistently communicated about God. Although general revelation may not be enough, we dare not deny it!

Think of this: Our solar system is about six billion miles across. And that's only *one* solar system! Our galaxy, the Milky Way, contains roughly four hundred billion stars. That is but one galaxy of what we now call metagalaxies. There are thousands upon thousands of galaxies like ours.

Earth is one of the smallest planets in the whole solar system, 25,000 miles in circumference. The sun is 1,300,000 times larger than this planet. We have now been able to explore with telescopes billions and quadrillions of miles of space. Yet we have been able to talk about, reason, and understand just a finite bit of what this solar system is.

Still, many men do not see the God who wants to speak about His own person, His own holiness, and His own power. He wants to speak to man through that very means. G. Studdard Kennedy, one of the great thinkers and writers of past generations, tells the story of his own conversion.

He said one night he was alone on a moor beside the sea. Above him was the great dome of heaven with millions of stars. There was no sound at all except the boom of waves against the cliff. But in that moment, he said, he became acutely conscious of Another, a vast mysterious Presence other than himself, moving in the dark among the tiny lights of the worlds above him. He said:

> I felt like crying out, "Who goes there?" I was reminded of a time during the war. On a battlefield in France I had lain down in a no man's land between the trenches. That night I saw a moving figure coming toward me in the semi-darkness. I didn't know whether it was a friend or an enemy. I whispered that night, "Who goes there?" not knowing whether the answer would be a bullet, or a friendly word, or silence. That is how I felt that night on the moor — alone with my thoughts and the sea. Who goes there? Was there an answer? I made my cry, and when I did, I got my answer. It is not that it has been perfect, or never doubted, or wholly understood, but it remains. If I lost it, I think I would lose my soul. I've been trying to say it ever since, one word. God. That night I stood in the presence of God.[10]

Who goes there? God's revelation — God's general revelation! Let me assure you, especially if you are overly concerned about your own responsibility, that when we pray and acknowledge the work of the Holy Spirit, we set God free to use every means to awaken in the spirit of man — however covered with dust and dirt — a cry of the heart of acknowledgment of God.

Of course, it isn't the end. The psalmist in Psalm 8 cries, "What is man? I see the work of Your hands. I see the work of Your fingers, this great moon and stars; but what is man that You are mindful of him, and the son of man that You visit him?" God has declared in His Word that He leads from faith to faith. The scriptures account for many ways in which God visits man. Two are obvious: direct *theophanies* and through sending Jesus Christ.

Someone said, *"God the Father walked down the ethereal staircase of heaven with a baby in His arms."* The Incarnation, which no man understands — in which God allowed Himself to be wrapped in flesh, to be touchable, human, and bruisable — was the ultimate desire of God to visit man.

God visits man by sending the Holy Spirit. God visits man by sending angels. God visits man by prophets. God visits man by dreams and visions. God visits most often through His Word; the Word itself. And God chooses to visit us through the preaching of the Word. There are those in every church who talk about the ineffectiveness of preaching. I hear people say, "We've had enough preaching. Let's have a moratorium on preaching until we begin to live what we know." It is the mystery of God's revelation, but it is a fact that God has chosen "the foolishness of preaching" to save those who will believe.

"Preaching" is an interesting word in the Greek language. It is the word *kerugma.* It means "to proclaim." Actually, it comes from the concept of a courier or a messenger running ahead of a king, blowing the trumpet and saying, "Hear ye, hear ye!"

We can talk about all of our psychological and modern means of presentation, but make no mistake: *God visits man through the Word.* He has chosen today, as He has for 2000 years, since the ultimate giving of Himself in Jesus Christ, to visit man by the preaching of the Word.

And here is a divine power. It has nothing to do with the character of a proclaimer. It has nothing to do with the life of the person who is proclaiming. There is a divine power in the Word so it will not return void unto God. It will accomplish the purpose to which it was sent. That word is incarnate of the Holy Spirit when it goes forth and God chooses to visit man.

The Psalms speak to our condition. Our concerns are perfectly matched by any encounter with God who confronts and comforts us. [11]

—Lloyd John Ogilvie

CHAPTER 13

Mankind's Purpose

I once taught a series from Psalm 8, and I had recently been revolutionized through my own study. A visiting minister who was present came to me afterwards and said, "The Holy Spirit really tore me apart this morning. The word you gave was right. I have spent a lifetime depreciating man, thinking I was doing God a favor."

You will remember that David writes as the introduction to Psalm 8, "To the chief Musician upon *Gittith,* A Psalm of David." *Gittith* probably referred to the geographical region of Gath. Perhaps this Psalm was to be sung on a musical instrument peculiar to the land of Gath. Just as likely, however, is the fact that Gath is the land from which Goliath came and the region in which David spent most of his time running from Saul, and it therefore had unusual memories for David.

Gath, in the Hebrew language, means "winepress." Needless to say, David had been in a lot of winepresses before he wrote this Psalm! From boyhood, David's winepresses had come in the shapes of lions, bears, contempt, giants, jealousy, and, finally, infinite delay in God's purpose for his life. Those were David's winepresses.

When he wrote this Psalm, we might paraphrase David's beginning as follows: "Listen, friends, this Psalm can only be sung on the basis of experience." It is as though David is saying, "The background of this music must be the reality of a personal winepress. When you sing this song, accompany its words with the grinding, gutsy reality of life."

In that sense, I really identify this Psalm with the words of the apostle Paul in Romans 5. You know this is the great chapter about feeling at home with God. It's the chapter about the application of justification by faith. Justification by faith is made practical and applies to our lives. It begins with these glorious words: "Therefore, having been justified by faith...." Two verses later we read, "...we also glory in tribulations, knowing that tribulation produces perseverance; and perseverance, character; and character, hope" (Romans 5:3,4).

The word "tribulation" in that scripture is the Greek word *thlipsis,* which means "pressure." An accurate translation might read, "Pressure works endurance, and endurance produces character, and character brings to birth hope." Continuing, Paul wrote, "Now hope does not disappoint, because the love of God has been poured out in our hearts by the Holy Spirit who was given to us" (verse 5).

The winepress is pressure. David's personal winepress brought him to grips with God and man. It brought him to reality with ultimate truth and pervading purpose so he could cry from his heart, "O Lord, our Lord, Yahweh Adonai, the Lord who is master of all, how excellent is Your name in all the earth." Then he would cry, "What is man — what is this mystery of man — that You care for him, that You are mindful of him, and that You visit him?"

Winepresses do that! Winepresses demand answers. What is life all about? Is there any real purpose? Is there life after birth? I guarantee you, if we had time to poll the average crowd in a church on Sunday morning, 70 percent of those who are born again of the Spirit of God became born again Christians as a result of some kind of a winepress.

If you are a Christian, you will probably agree with that. God turned the screws on your life. Things you were looking to in your own life didn't work out. There was a time of pressure. The winepress became the moment of your looking up into personal identity with who God is and what His purpose really is for you.

Barbra Streisand sings an interesting song which she made famous. The words go like this:

Where am I going? Why should I care?
No matter where I run, I meet myself there.
Looking inside me, what do I see?
Anger and hope and doubt.
What am I all about, and where am I going?[12]

In a sense, that's where the message of Palm 8 begins. First there is a fervent plea that you understand man. Not man from the perspective of Genesis 3 — the distortion of sin and the results of rebellion which occurred from the Fall — but that you go back and include in your understanding Genesis 1. It seems to argue that you must see man from the perspective of divine creation.

Psalm 8 is saying that man is capable of recognizing, when anointed by the Holy Spirit, God's very character and workmanship, and man's unique destiny found in God's ultimate purpose and glory.

God made man in His own image — and, however distorted, however perverted, however sinful man becomes — man has stamped upon his inner self the borrowed breath of God. But all this truth of recognition must be quickly modified. Man also has a built-in receiver. He can receive truth. He cannot invent or discover that truth for himself, however. God *must* reveal it. Romans 1:17 says "...the righteousness of God is revealed...." And verses 19 and 20 say:

because what may be known of God is manifest in them, for God has shown it to them.

For since the creation of the world His invisible attributes are clearly seen, being understood by the things that are made, even His eternal power and Godhead, so that they are without excuse.

Similarly, Psalm 19 says:

The heavens declare the glory of God; and the firmament shows His handiwork.

Day unto day utters speech, and night unto night reveals knowledge [mystery].

> **There is no speech nor language where their voice is not heard.**
>
> **Their line has gone out through all the earth, and their words to the end of the world.**
>
> **Psalm 19:1-4 *NKJV***

This world has had a Teacher who cannot fail in His work. That is the Holy Spirit. But Romans 1 also says that this revelation is from faith to faith; it's progressive. A man must take the first step if he is to get to the second.

Psalm 19, "the general revelation," as theologians call it — the revelation of creation — isn't enough for a man to be born of the Spirit. It is but a platform, but if a man will take that step to see God, God will move him on to the second step.

David cries in Psalm 8, "When I consider Your heavens, the work of Your fingers, the moon and the stars, which You have ordained, What is man...?" He begins with that. God will lead him, cycle by cycle, full cycle unto Himself in His own righteousness. That is God's promise.

People can talk about the lost of Africa and those tribes who have never heard the Gospel, but God's declaration is that there is nowhere that first message is *not* declared. Furthermore, if any man responds to it, God promises to lead him to the next step. Both history and missions anthologies document the response of this. God has and does reveal Himself.

Let us never forget or compromise our inevitable step of revelation. There is a clue within the spirit of man that gives the mystery away. It is a key in man's own spirit which constantly demands to be turned. Listen again to these words from Psalm 8:5,6:

> **For You have made him a little lower than the angels, and You have crowned him with glory and honor.**
>
> **You have made him to have dominion over the works of Your hands; You have put all things under his feet.**

I believe there is an ultimate evangelical fear of this truth! The fear is revealed by the translation of verse 5. It may be the most unanimously *mistranslated* verse in the Bible! Could it be that the mistranslation comes out of the prejudice of our hearts? We simply can't believe it says what it does.

The original Hebrew says clearly, "O God, what is man that thou art mindful of him? *Thou hast made him a little lower than Elohim." Elohim*, of course, is the word of Genesis 1: "In the beginning *Elohim* created the heavens and the earth." The word *Elohim*, the plural in the word "God," appears thousands of times throughout the Old Testament.

It was always translated "God," except when the Greek Septuagint translators came to Psalm 8. To be honest, how can we believe that God is saying through David, "You have made man a little lower than *God"?* A little lower than divinity! Man is *not* lower than angels; that's heresy. Angels are ministering spirits sent to minister to those who inherit salvation (Hebrews 1:14).

No one who studies the scripture believes that man is lower than angels. God has put a borrowed part of His own nature in man. Man has the ability of volition and choice, the will by which he can determine destiny. We all know that. But for some reason we cannot come to grips with what is really said: *Man is just lower than divinity and has been given dominion* (verse 6). It would be amazing to read the average commentator on this passage. It's incredible! It quickly shows how diseased we are in our understanding on this subject.

Remember, there's an inveterate rumor — a word that won't go away — which is whispered, even in the hog pen, even in man's sinfulness, even in the most debauched corners of man's perverse understanding of himself. That whisper won't go away. It says that *man is somebody. He has a destiny in the stars!* He is meant to be something important! It has been said by more than one person, "Every man wants to play Hamlet." And that's not a coincidence.

Some years ago, a nondescript man caught in the humdrum of life, who had never done anything significant or important, went to the World's Fair in Chicago. A reporter saw the little man two years later, and he was still wearing proudly on his lapel a giant-sized button that said, "I ATTENDED THE CENTURY OF PROGRESS." He was somebody! He had become important! There is something inside all of us wanting to be taken out of the humdrum, to do something of significance, and to become important.

I'm sure you've read Mark Twain's stories. You remember that Tom Sawyer's dreams all came out the same way: He was *important*. Somehow or other Tom played "The Drum Major." He was the character who came home from the war riding the great charger and found Becky Thatcher, with her lovely curls and soft eyes, cheering him on as the returning hero. I believe it was J. Wallace Hamilton, a famous Presbyterian pastor, who called this "The Drum Major Instinct."

I recently received a letter from a publisher beginning a new magazine. In the first paragraph, the manager of this new publication began his letter by saying, "As you undoubtedly know, your name is on several mailing lists in which you are classified as highly literate, progressive, interested in world affairs, good literature, and science." There it is — it's in all of us! Psalm 8:4,5 really says, *"God, I don't understand it, but You have made man just a little lower than Yourself!"*

I love stories about Irish women. My mother was an Irish woman. Indeed, she fit many of the stereotypes of Irish women in general. There is a story about a census taker who came to a little Irish woman and said, "Lady, I'm taking a census. What's your name, and how many children do you have?"

She began by saying, "Well, let me see...there's Marcia, Michael, Dougie, Amy, Patrick..." He said, "Never mind the *names*, lady! Just give me the *numbers*."

She put her hands on her hips, straightened up to her full height, and with an Irish twinkle in her eye said, "I'll have you know, sir, we ain't got to numberin' 'em yet. We ain't run out of names."

Perhaps that's a classic illustration of the differences in our world. To some people, man is not a name; he's a number. Even some evangelicals haven't settled whether man is someone who counts, or he's simply someone to be counted. One thing emerges sharply from all New Testament literature and really from throughout the whole Bible. It is the *dignity* of man, the *sacredness* of human personality, the *infinite worth* of the human soul. It's on every page of the Bible.

You may call Psalm 8 "Hebrew poetry," and it is. You may say it is just a simple-hearted shepherd watching his flock getting carried away in a rapturous moment and pouring out an emotional burst. But *it's divine truth!* The Old and New Testaments confirm that man is created in the image of God. He is crowned with glory and honor. That supreme concern of God in all the universe is *man*.

Today with the revelations of astronomers, many people find their faith has been shattered. They count new stars, or talk about megagalaxies, and mankind drifts into insignificance. Others get involved in the philosophies or the political ideologies of man.

The media thinks in terms of collectivisms, and computers reduce us to table numbers. Others get caught up in man's history, his endless wars and perversities, his cruelties, and his stupidities. No doubt they're there! God knows they're there. But you dare not misunderstand the conclusion. The God who fashioned man made him a little less than Himself, and crowned him with honor, dignity, and meaning.

Dr. Iddings Bell once wrote — and I think it is one of the most profound statements I've read — "There are many ways of saying what's wrong with the world, but as penetrating as any is that which says that man is about to perish on this planet because he's lost the vision of his true greatness to such an extent that he's become scarcely more than a self-destructive animal."[13] Many of us have played into the hands of that satanic lie! Man does become bestial and animal-like when he loses his sense of connection with the destiny of who he is.

There once was a weaver in Edinburgh, Scotland, who purportedly had a prayer he prayed as though he was praying against all the forces which would crush his soul: "O Lord, help me to have a high opinion of myself."

When I was a young man, I was rebellious and did all I could to run from the call of God and the claims of my family. My dad would stand at the door as I was leaving for the evening, not to ask me where I was going in some legalistic caging of my spirit, but he would catch my eye and say, "Son, remember, you're a Christian, and you're a Howard." *And I would go out to try to have fun with that in my mind!* Lord, help me to have a high opinion of myself!

Man stands halfway between an atom and a star. He is the most ingenious mechanism that has ever been put together. Perhaps some generally known statistics might be reviewed here.

Our body has 263 bones, 600 muscles, and 970 miles of blood vessels. There are 400 cups on the tongue alone which help us taste and 20,000 hairs in the ear, which sound every sound separately. The jaw pressure of the human head is 40 pounds. There are 10,000 nerves with their branches and 35,000 sweat tubes. If you laid them out side by side, they would be more than 40 miles long. The intestines have 20 million small mouths which translate food into life. Our lungs enable a person to take in 24 gallons of air every day. What a mechanism! What a device!

Without question, God testifies to us about the sense of ultimate purpose. Man is a mixture. From the day of his birth until his death, he is a little bit of heaven, and he is a little bit of Earth. But never forget that the question "What is man?" has a Christian answer to it. Man is a child of Earth and a child of eternity. Human life is a curious mixture of dust and deity, of frailty and humanity.

Man is crowned by his Creator. He is only a little less than divine! That means something — something about the way I treat myself — and it means something about the attitude I have toward the world of mankind. There is a divine confidence placed upon man. God has never looked upon mankind cheaply. Some people may think that the preacher's business is to rail at people about their sins. I believe, in contrast, that we need a postgraduate course to tell people just who they are and who God has made them! God knows us, and God loves us!

John Wesley, the great English evangelist, was an interesting personality. He used to make little notes about each sermon he had preached. It is reported that he wrote in one such note, "I preached to some miners today. My text was, 'As many as received him, to them he gave the power to become the sons of God.'" Wesley's comment was, "They seemed greatly encouraged."

Another great and gifted preacher of England relates that as a college youth he was wayward and unruly. His family had unanimously predicted that he would "go bad." He was just resentful enough to determine that he would live up to their expectations!

Isn't that the course of life for many of us? When we were 5 or 6, someone said we were "a dumb, stupid kid," and we've been proving it for 25 or 30 years! Or we heard someone say that we were ugly or lazy, so we are.

This young man meant to prove it. One evening, after coming away from an evening of debauchery, he was creeping up the stairs to his bedroom, shoes in hand, when a door opened into the hallway. His grandmother was standing there with a lighted candle, and she put her ancient hand on his shoulder and said five words that changed his life: *"John, I believe in you!"* During those night hours, in the darkness of his room, with his head in his hands, the miracle of a re-found life came to pass.

God believes in you! How can anyone trek up Golgotha and see the innocent Son of God dying the ignominious death of Calvary, with His own blood drenching His body, and believe anything less than that? God places a high value on man. God cares! God is mindful of us!

Before leaving this section of Psalm 8, please note verses 6 through 8:

You have made him to have dominion over the works of Your hands; You have put all things under his feet,

All sheep and oxen — even the beasts of the field,

The birds of the air, and the fish of the sea that pass through the paths of the seas.

How do you express what is said in these verses? It is as though the writer says, "There's something in my spirit that tells me I was made to have dominion." In other words, God dignified man by weaving into his nature the mysterious gift of freedom, saying, "Thou hast made man to be free." Every scheme of political dominion which has come around in the 6000 recorded years of man's history could never ultimately succeed in quenching this spiritual inner man which says, "I'm made to be free. I'm not the slave of anyone." Some people think freedom is political. It isn't, really; it's spiritual!

I once was told the following parable about creation. God made a whole bunch of little "seeds of life" and asked them to choose what they would be. Some wanted to be elephants or tigers. Some wanted to be in the water, so God gave them fins to swim, and thus made fish. Others wanted more air than water, so He gave them wings to fly. The parable continued, some were concerned about safety and security, and He gave them shells to carry on their backs.

Finally, after all the little seeds had spoken, just one was left. According to this parable, in humility it said, "I don't want wings or fins. Just let me be in Your image. I'll make my own wings, boats, and houses. Just make me in Your image, and I'll take my chance with that." And, the parable says, God was well pleased and made man.

Run as far as you want. Turn the music up so loud, you seemingly will never again be able to hear anything from God. But the truth is in the human spirit that God made and gave to you: You are not meant to be a slave but a son. *You are not destined for the hog pen; you are destined for the stars!*

Some Christians are unhappy with an emphasis like these last two chapters. There is a third reality in this Psalm that is not completed until the New Testament. For example, the writer of Hebrews quoted this Psalm and then said, "...but now we do not yet see all things put under his feet" (Hebrews 2:8). Whose feet — Jesus' feet? Certainly all things are ultimately under His feet. But that is not the context. The context is man! Man!

The story of the Fall in Genesis 3 is that when man rebelled and sinned, God came that very day to walk in the Garden in the coolness of the day to have fellowship with man. The Bible says that God called to Adam and asked him, "Where are you?"

Perhaps some of us, in our anthropomorphic ideas of God, think that God in this story is like a mother running around looking through the closets, shouting, "Where are you, Johnny?" God knew where they were. He knew when the sin originated in their hearts! In Genesis 3, God is saying, "Man, it's important that *you* understand where you are and what has brought you to this place."

Man through transgression fell. He was deceived by the enemy of God, the accuser, the avenger; deceived by this ultimate enemy of truth. Man crumbled from dominion. He lost his freedom. He became the servant of sin. He who commits sin is the servant or slave of sin.

Man was driven from the Garden of Eden — from the place of position of his ultimate purpose — from dominion over the earth. What's more, he suffered the loss of fellowship with God. Many of us are uncomfortable with incongruities. We want to solve everything neatly. Man is either depraved, or we have the universal brotherhood of man and the Fatherhood of God. We are uncomfortable with dichotomies and uncomfortable with balance. Granted, there is an element of inconsistency.

I once heard about a man who wrote a book about women. That was a mistake. He wrote the book when he was young — probably the only time anyone would tackle such a subject! Some years later when he came to know more about his subject, he decided to re-publish the book. However, instead of going through the material to revise it, he simply wrote a blanket correction on the preface page. It read as follows: "Wherever in this volume appears the word 'is,' substitute 'is not.' And wherever the word 'is not' appears, substitute 'maybe,' 'perhaps,' or 'God only knows.'"

So much for consistency! There's an element of inconsistency between that breathing of the Spirit of God in man which says who he is and where he's destined to be and between the sin, the transgression, and the Fall. The Fall was real! Its effects are pronounced and obvious. Mankind became separated from God, depraved in nature, ignorant and blind, evil in conscience, corrupt and deceitful in heart, and obstinate and rebellious. He became lustful and ungodly, dominated by Satan, the servant of sin — in fact, dead in sin — and doomed to eternity without God or hope.

Man had now fallen short of the glory of God, was subject to suffering, and was cursed by God to hard labor. He was mortal, imperfect, weak, and universally sinful! The Fall was real! But the reality of the Fall simply accentuates the original purpose. It makes all the more real the longing that says, "Hey, I meant to go somewhere. I meant to be something!"

Everything about our life says something is wrong. Man's spirit attests to who he is and what he should be. Yet he is not what he's supposed to be. There's a missing link. He must trust the Holy Spirit to complete his understanding of Psalm 8. The Old Testament is explained in the New Testament, and the Old Testament is revealed in the New Testament.

The second chapter of Hebrews is a continuing revelation. It begins with a warning concerning the danger of neglecting so great a salvation. Then the writer continues:

> **For He has not put the world to come, of which we speak, in subjection to angels.**

> But one testified in a certain place, saying: "What is man that You are mindful of him, Or the son of man that You take care of him?
>
> You made him a little lower than the angels; You crowned him with glory and honor, And set him over the works of Your hands.
>
> You have put all things in subjection under his feet."
>
> Hebrews 2:5-8 *NKJV*

Following this direct quote from Psalm 8:4-6 (direct although using the Greek word "angels" rather than the Hebrew *Elohim*, as previously mentioned), the writer continues his point:

> For in that He put all in subjection under him, He left nothing that is not put under him. *But now we do not yet see all things* put under him.
>
> But we see Jesus, who was made a little lower than the angels, for the suffering of death crowned with glory and honor, that He, by the grace of God, might taste death for everyone.
>
> Hebrews 2:8,9 *NKJV*

We don't see man in dominion. We don't see man fulfilled in the image of God — *but we do see Jesus!* Here is revelation indeed. Before turning from Hebrews 2, we should note some other phrases later in that chapter.

This Jesus is "the author [or first-goer] of this salvation." Perhaps no section of the Bible is more necessary for our understanding of mankind than Hebrews 2:14-18 *(NKJV)*:

> Inasmuch then as the children have partaken of flesh and blood, He Himself likewise shared in the same, that through death He might destroy him who had the power of death, that is, the devil,
>
> and release those who through fear of death were all their lifetime subject to bondage.
>
> For indeed He does not give aid to angels, but He does give aid to the seed of Abraham.

173

Therefore, in all things He had to be made like His brethren, that He might be a merciful and faithful High Priest in things pertaining to God, to make propitiation for the sins of the people.

For in that He Himself has suffered, being tempted, He is able to aid those who are tempted.

Psalm 8 is not an abnormality. When David cries, "What is man that You are mindful of him, and the son of man that You visit him?" (verse 4), he was participating in divine revelation through the gift of human recognition. The Hebrew word "mindful" in Psalm 8 is *zakar*. It means to constantly have your attention. Scholars suggest that the literal means something like incense coming up continually before one's presence, or, again, to have one's mind constantly turned toward a certain object. That is what God is toward you. God has, like incense rising before Him, His mind constantly on man!

No man can understand the exciting vulnerability of the psalmists without a clear understanding of this truth from Psalm 8. God's purpose and intention is not illustrated by a yo-yo. We don't discover His intention by petal-plucking, "He loves me, He loves me not; He loves me, He loves me not..." God will not have His plan ultimately thwarted. Mankind is His permanent focus.

True psalmists live intimately with one another and with God in spite of their failures, momentary loss of focus, and even spiritual anger. They trust in a foundational, unconditional purpose and direction. They know God, and they trust Him.

The word "redemption" has almost become lost to us in the wrangles of theology. It always means "to buy back" or receive back something which originally belonged to you. The three principles of redemption in the Old Testament were: (1) to redeem property lost by default; (2) to redeem persons sold into slavery out of poverty, and (3) to redeem by means of reproduction a family name lost because of the premature death of the head of the family.

God sent Jesus Christ, His Son, to live a perfect, sinless life and to die on the cross of Calvary. There was an enormous price to undo what mankind had done by rebellion. It was to re-exercise a second validity on His created ownership of us, that by redemption we would be His, as we had always been His by creation.

Romans 3:24,25 *(NKJV)* reads:

being justified freely by His grace through the redemption that is in Christ Jesus,

whom God set forth to be a *propitiation* by His blood, through faith, to demonstrate His righteousness, because in His forbearance God had passed over the sins that were previously committed.

"Propitiation" is the word for "mercy seat." Jesus Christ, according to this scripture, has been made a propitiation for us, meaning "sacrifice on the mercy seat." "Propitious" means "to have good intentions and high desires; to have good purposes for someone." To be "propitious" toward you means that all my intentions and desires toward you are good!

Through Jesus Christ on the cross outside Jerusalem in a specific point in history and time, God's Son became the propitiation for all mankind. That means that *God is no longer mad at anyone!* It doesn't matter who we are or what we've done. There will never be another Calvary. The propitiation took place *once* in history. Again, the writer of Hebrews says:

...but now, once at the end of the ages, He has appeared to put away sin by the sacrifice of Himself.

Hebrews 9:26 *NKJV*

It's *never* going to happen again in history. When it happened, and from that moment on, God was *thoroughly* satisfied with the sacrifice of His Son. He is not angry at man anymore; however, reconciliation is a two-way street.

I think of many friends and others who are living in open rebellion against God, destroying their bodies and minds. Often they are motivated by a stereotyped image of God (one we've often given them in the church): God, with a big stick...God, who's ready to kick His kids out of the family every time they fail.

They are running. They are unhappy, knowing their ultimate purpose and destiny is unfulfilled, yet going farther and farther away from God into a pit of despair. God is running after them, His arms wide open, saying, "I'm not angry! It's already been paid! I'm not mad at you! I've been reconciled to you. Now will *you* be reconciled to Me?"

There is a popular Christian song which says, "He was there all the time, waiting patiently in line." The song speaks about a person doing all his own things, using relationships, with things out of line, doing things wrong, getting involved in purposeless living. Here's God saying, "I've been reconciled to you. The propitiation has been paid. I'm not angry with you. Now reconcile yourself to Me. Sign the peace treaty I've already signed in the blood of My Son. Agree to the terms I've already agreed to."

I've always thought it revealing what the apostle Paul wrote in Romans 15:7: "Therefore receive one another, just as Christ also received us, to the glory of God." This verse comes in the context of a two-chapter discussion concerning believers' relationships. There was an abundance of judgment going on over individual believers' convictions. Paul spoke of their "contempt," of "stumbling blocks," and of the possibility of destroying the work of God over personal scruples.

But it appears to me that Romans 15:7 is a two-edged sword. We might define its logic in two simple syllogisms:

1. The believer's relationship with other believers is to be determined by the sacrificial, unconditional manner in which God has accepted us through the sacrifice of Jesus Christ; not by or through performance or waiting for proof, but according to faith.

2. The believer must be thoroughly aware and truly convinced of the completeness and unconditional nature of God's acceptance of him through faith in Jesus Christ in order that

his relationships with other believers will duplicate his knowledge of how God received him.

The world is comfortable with the Psalms. It is the leading devotional resource of three of the world's greatest religions: Christianity, Judaism, and Islam. While most literature in the faith of those three groups divides and frustrates each other, the Psalms unite them!

Our task in this book has been simple: to discover and illustrate how the Psalms provide a laboratory for open, honest, and yet revealing personal faith. We have suggested that the philosophy of the psalmists allows not only for non-deceptive and vulnerable lifestyle, but also provides the basis for a true believer's community, which is transparent, struggling, open, and inviting.

We have chosen in this book to deal only with the first eight psalms, because they seem a recognized unit in both the life of David and as an illustration of the true approach and access to God, which is freeing, non-defensive, and open to experiential change.

Faith in God is faith with God. Theology can no more be simply knowledge than can driving a car or making love. Intimacy is more than a word written on a blackboard. It must be lived out in crisis and trust, fear, and security. It is my belief that principles and understandings from this book are provable. They wait the personal authentication of the laboratory — the laboratory of *your* life.

[1]F. J. E. Woodbridge, as quoted by Harold A. Bosley, op. cit., p. 16.

[2]Willem A. VanGemeren, *Psalms, The Expositor's Bible Commentary*. Zondervan, Grand Rapids, 1991, p. 6.

[3]C. S. Lewis, *Reflections on the Psalms*, p. 134

[4]I am reminded of a scene from Franco Zeffirelli's film "Brother Sun, Sister Moon" (Euro-International Films, 1972), in which Alec Guiness as Innocent III gives his papal blessing to Saint Francis of Assisi with the words, "In our obsession with original sin, we too often forget original innocence."

[5]Fanny J. Crosby, "Rescue the Perishing," public domain.

[6]Leon Bloy, as quoted by Harold L. Bosley, op. cit., p. 6.

[7]Arnold J. Toynbee, *A Study of History*. Oxford Uiversity Press, Volume V, pp. 16,17.

[8]Jean Paul Richter, as qujoted by J. Wallace Hamilton, *Who Goes There? What and Where Is God?* Fleming H. Revell Company. Old Tappan, New Jersey, 1958, p. 13.

[9]Mark Twain, op. cit.

[10]G. Studdard Kennedy, as quoted by J. Wallace Hamilton, op. cit., pp. 11,12.

[11]Lloyd John Ogilvie, op. cit., p. 12.

[12]"Where Am I Going" (Cy Coleman, Dorothy Fields) (c) 1965, 1969 Notable Music Co., Inc. & Lida Enterprises, Inc. All rights administered by WB Music Corp. All rights reserved. Used by permission.

[13]Dr. Iddings Bell, as quoted by J. Wallace Hamilton, op cit., p. 74.

Suggested Readings in the Psalms

*A*fter many years, C. H. Spurgeon's abundant work *The Treasury of David* is still to be recommended and used. It is available in many forms, from single- to multiple-volume editions.

For direct modern research, the reader is encouraged to read *The Expositor's Bible Commentary*, Frank E. Gaebelein, General Editor. Even more technical understandings from a modern perspective can be found in the *Word Biblical Commentary* series, volumes 19, 20, and 21.

Again, for an older but excellent series, consult the often-republished *The Pulpit Commentary*, volume 8 on the Psalms. Also consult the more-difficult-to-find books *Meditations in the Psalms* by Erling C. Olsen and Arno C. Gaebelein's *The Book of Psalms*.

The Communicator's Commentary, of which Lloyd J. Ogilvie is general editor, contains two excellent volumes on the Psalms, volumes 13 and 14. There are similar volumes in all commentary sets and other simple study books.

Above all, read the Psalms. They in themselves are letters of life.

Christ Is the Secret of the Psalms

Someone else is praying, not me... The One who is here protesting His Innocence, who is invoking God's judgment, who has come to such infinite depths of suffering, is none other than Jesus Christ Himself. He it is who is praying here, and not only here but in the whole Psalter.

— Dietrich Bonhoeffer
Life Together
Harper & Row,
New York, p. 31.

The publication of *Songs From Life* has been encouraged by the generosity of Don and Deanna Duffy, Ken and Roberta Eldred, Jill and Vishaal Mathur and, as always, by Janet Pomeroy, a founder and mentor of Naioth Sound and Publishing.

Naioth Sound and Publishing
2995 Woodside Road, Suite 400
Woodside, California 94062

Toll free: 1-800-726-3127
Fax: 1-415-368-0790

Discounts for volume amounts:
40% Discount for bookstores
50% Discount for churches
60% Discount for distributors